WORLD BANK STAFF OCCASIONAL PAPERS NUMBER TEN

WORLD BANK STAFF OCCASIONAL PAPERS NUMBER TEN

SHLOMO REUTLINGER

TECHNIQUES FOR PROJECT APPRAISAL UNDER UNCERTAINTY

Published for the World Bank by
THE JOHNS HOPKINS UNIVERSITY PRESS
Baltimore and London

Copyright © 1970 by the International Bank
for Reconstruction and Development / THE WORLD BANK
1818 H Street, N.W., Washington, D.C. 20433, U.S.A.
All rights reserved
Manufactured in the United States of America

The Johns Hopkins University Press
Baltimore, Maryland 21218, U.S.A.

Originally published 1970
Second printing 1972
Third printing 1976
Fourth printing 1979
Fifth printing 1984

Library of Congress Catalog Card Number 74–94827
ISBN 0-8018-1154-6

FOREWORD

I would like to explain why the World Bank does research work and why this research is published. We feel an obligation to look beyond the projects that we help to finance toward the whole resource allocation of an economy and the effectiveness of the use of those resources. Our major concern, in dealings with member countries, is that all scarce resources—including capital, skilled labor, enterprise, and know-how—should be used to their best advantage. We want to see policies that encourage appropriate increases in the supply of savings, whether domestic or international. Finally, we are required by our Articles, as well as by inclination, to use objective economic criteria in all our judgments.

These are our preoccupations, and these, one way or another, are the subjects of most of our research work. Clearly, they are also the proper concern of anyone who is interested in promoting development, and so we seek to make our research papers widely available. In doing so, we have to take the risk of being misunderstood. Although these studies are published by the Bank, the views expressed and the methods explored should not necessarily be considered to represent the Bank's views or policies. Rather, they are offered as a modest contribution to the great discussion on how to advance the economic development of the underdeveloped world.

ROBERT S. McNAMARA
President
The World Bank

TABLE OF CONTENTS

TABLES

FIGURES

PREFACE

This study is concerned with the appraisal of events which have uncertain outcomes. This issue is generally recognized, but is usually not explicitly considered in otherwise detailed cost-benefit analysis of investment projects. Application of contingency allowances and sensitivity analyses have been used as partial remedies. However, for the most part, project benefits are still estimated and reported in terms of one single outcome which does not take account of, or record, valuable information about the extent of uncertainty of project-related events.

This paper recommends that the best available judgments about the various factors underlying the cost and benefit estimates of the project be recorded in terms of probability distributions and that these distributions be aggregated in a mathematically correct manner to yield a probability distribution of the rate of return, or net present worth, of the project. This procedure in no way eliminates the problem of making judgments about events and relationships in the face of limited and incomplete information, nor does it suggest a unique and simple formula for choosing among projects or project strategies with varying degrees of riskiness. However, this type of analysis would ensure and encourage that available information about events affecting the outcome of the project would be more fully utilized and correctly transformed into information about uncertain project results. Project-related decisions could be made more easily and more intelligently if returns on projects were reported not in terms of a single rate, or a wide range of possible returns with undefined likelihoods of occurrence, but in terms of a probability distribution.

The present paper should be viewed primarily as providing a conceptual framework for further study into the scope and limitations of practical application of probability appraisal and pursuant project decisions. Several case studies are currently being investigated in the Bank by Louis Pouliquen and Tariq Husain. The author has benefited from many discussions with them. The author also wishes to acknowledge helpful comments by Herman G. van der Tak and Jan de Weille of the Sector and Project Group in the Economics Department and written comments on an earlier draft of this paper by Bank staff members: Messrs. B. Balassa, L. Goreux, A. Kundu, M. Schrenk, A. E. Tiemann, D. J. Wood of the Economics Department; and D. S. Ballantine, I. T. Friedgut, V. W. Hogg, P. O. Malone, H. P. Muth, M. Palein, S. Y. Park, M. Piccagli, L. Pouliquen, A. P. Pusar, V. Rajagopalan, S. Takahashi, V. Wouters of the Projects Department. However, the views expressed in this paper are those of the author, and he alone is responsible for them.

A. M. KAMARCK
Director
Economics Department

PART I

PROBABILITY ANALYSIS

I

INTRODUCTION

The primary purpose of this study is to present a feasible method for evaluating the riskiness of investment projects. A second objective is to show how quantitative evaluations of the riskiness of projects might be used in various decision problems. Throughout, the emphasis is on methodology and problems of measurement, not on description of various kinds of uncertainty problems, nor is much attention paid to theories which have no immediate applicability to project appraisal. Uncertainty is everywhere, as anyone knows; hence, a general descriptive study of uncertainty is unnecessary and the specific sources of uncertainty must be identified for each specific case. In general, however, the uncertainty conditions relevant for this study are those unique to a particular project, and not to "global" uncertainties which affect the outcomes of all projects within a country.

This study does not recommend a specific "best" attitude for a public investment authority or an international lending agency with respect to undertaking projects with uncertain outcomes. To do so, would be as presumptuous as to advise a government on the income distribution or the composition of goods and services it should promote for internal consumption. The pursuit of economic development is clearly inconsistent with a policy of avoiding all risks (there simply are no worthwhile projects without risks). At the other extreme, most people would agree that a project which

1

has a reasonably high probability of turning out badly should not be undertaken if that outcome would mean a considerable deterioration of the present economic well-being of a country. However, between those two extreme choices lie many alternatives whose desirability would depend on the *subjective* preferences or aversions to risk of the decision makers and their constituents.

This study deals at length with the question of how to evaluate and present in summary form a measure of the relative riskiness of projects, on the general assumption that a "good" judgment of risk is an important ingredient for reaching a "best" decision. For all practical purposes, decisions involving choices among uncertain economic returns from investment have one thing in common: they ask for judgments about the likelihood of the measure of returns used in the evaluation. For some the most relevant measure of returns is "the most likely one" (the mode). Others use exclusively a conservative estimate, that is one which has a "high chance of being exceeded," and still others wish to consider an entire set of returns, and their respective likelihoods.[1]

No attempt is made in this study to present a comprehensive review of all decision theories dealing with uncertainty. Such comprehensive reviews are available elsewhere.[2] They are useful to students and research workers but more often than not they leave the practitioner's problem unresolved. Only a small set of uncertainty hypotheses and decision criteria are presented in this paper.[3] They reflect, in the judgment of the author, the most

---

[1] Or as Marshak has stated it: "Instead of assuming an individual who thinks he knows the future events, we assume an individual who thinks he knows the probabilities of future events. We may call this situation the situation of a game of chance, and consider it as a better although still incomplete approximation to reality than the usual assumption that people believe themselves to be prophets." (J. Marshak, "Money and the Theory of Assets," *Econometrica*, 1938).

[2] See, for example: K. J. Arrow, "Alternative Approaches to the Theory of Choice in Risk-Taking Situations," *Econometrica*, 19:404–437 (1951); M. Friedman and L. T. Savage, "The Utility Analysis of Choice Involving Risk," *Journal of Political Economy*, LVI (August 1948); R. Dorfman, "Basic Economic and Technologic Concepts," A. Maas, *et al.*, *Design of Water Resource Systems*, Harvard University Press, 1962; D. E. Farrar, *The Investment Decision Under Uncertainty*, Prentice-Hall, 1962.

[3] The point of view taken in this study parallels most nearly the way F. Modigliani and K. J. Cohen have stated it: ". . . Probably the best available tool at this stage is the so-called 'expected-utility' theory . . . starting from certain basic postulates of rational behaviour this theory shows that the information available to the agent concerning an uncertain event can be represented by a 'subjective' probability distribution and that there exists a (cardinal) utility function such

useful and generally correct approaches to a large number of problems arising in project appraisal.

The commonly accepted procedure in project evaluation calls for the calculation of the return from each project and for criteria by which to choose from among different projects on the basis of the estimated returns.[4] The essence of the uncertainty problem is simply that many of the variables affecting the outcome of a particular plan of action are not controllable by the planner or decision-maker.[5] Hence project evaluation which takes due account of uncertainty involves (a) judgments about the likelihood of occurrence of the non-controllable variables, (b) calculation of a whole *set* of possible outcomes or returns for each project, and (c) criteria for choosing among projects on the basis of sets of possible returns from each project.

Chapter II assesses briefly the nature of uncertainty and the kind of judgments which are basic ingredients for the decision making process. Particular attention is paid to the notion that the uncertainty which is relevant for most decisions is best characterized in terms of a decision agent's subjective beliefs about the likelihoods of occurrence of various outcomes of the uncertain event. Such probability distributions may be based, of course, on more or less evidence and in this sense might be labeled more or less "objective."[6] While for any given event it may be desirable to marshall more evidence, if this is possible and not too costly, here we postulate that for reaching a decision it makes little difference whether an event is "known" in terms of a more subjective or a more objective probability distribution. It would be a sad mistake to subscribe to a decision theory which fails to consider variables simply because their outcomes or probability distributions of outcomes are not known with certainty. Errors of omission could be more important than errors of commission. Only quantifiable "objective" evidence would then be admitted. What matters is only whether an event has important consequences for a decision, and

---

that the agent acts as though he were endeavoring to maximise the expected value of his utility . . ." ("The Significance and Uses of Ex Ante Data," in *Expectations, Uncertainty and Business Behavior*, edited by M. J. Bowman, New York, Social Science Research Council, 1958).

[4] The criteria are for the most part derived from a deterministic model which assumes that the exact returns are known.

[5] Such non-controllable variables might be prices, incomes, population, size of labor force and climate. While governments may have some control over some of these variables, they are not likely to be interested or to succeed in controlling them completely.

[6] Of course we do postulate that the source of the judgment is an expert acting without prejudice and in good faith.

not how "objective" or "subjective" the estimate or probability distribution of its outcome is.[7]

Among the various characterizations of uncertainty advocated by different theories, the probabilistic approach has been singled out primarily because this lends itself best to an appraisal of the possible outcomes of a project which is affected by uncertainties from many different sources. It is shown how probability judgments about many basic variables and parameters affecting the final outcome of a project can be aggregated into an estimate of the probability distribution of that final outcome. The advantages of "building up" such an estimate are many: (a) it is generally easier to formulate judgments about the outcomes of basic events than about the outcomes from a project because such events are frequently recurring, whereas projects are usually unique in some respect, (b) the outcomes of events, such as rainfall, production functions or prices are likely to be evaluated with less emotional bias and more factual evidence than a project's overall benefits, (c) judgments about the outcomes of various "simple" events utilize the experience of many experts who should be in the best position to know, and, finally, (d) analytical insights into the desirability of restructuring a project can be gained from knowledge of the specific contribution of each underlying factor to the probability distribution of the project's final outcome.

The "subjective" definition of probability implies at once that the process of estimation is both an art and a science. The quality of judgments involved in estimation will vary with the nature of the variables and the appraiser's expertise in interpolating and extrapolating related observations and experience. Quite generally, desirable prerequisites for good judgments are (a) knowledge of past outcomes of the event (experience and data), (b) knowledge of basic relationships which could explain why the outcomes of the event might have varied in the past and how they might vary in the future (a model), and (c) sound procedures for interpreting the interaction of model and data (statistics). To the extent that formal theory, subject matter expertise, and analytical tools can assist in the estimation process, they are assumed to be known to project appraisers and are not elaborated in this study.

---

[7] In the terminology suggested by Frank Knight, events whose probability distributions can be objectively known are sometimes labeled as "risks," and subjectively conceived distributions are called "uncertainties." The point of view taken in this study is that this is not a meaningful classification, both because there are no "subjective" but only more or less "objective" estimates, and because the extent of objectivity does not necessarily alter their interpretation in terms of decisions. (F. H. Knight, *Risk Uncertainty and Profit*, Boston, Houghton Mifflin Co., 1921.)

Chapter III discusses how to aggregate probability distributions of relevant factors and parameters into a probability distribution of the economic returns of a project. The problems arising when uncertain estimates of the various factors are combined have been for the most part neglected or inadequately treated by conventional appraisal methods, although for these aggregation problems at least it is possible to prescribe a uniquely correct methodology. The factors one chooses to consider in any economic appraisal of a project, and the prediction of their outcomes and estimations of how they interrelate are always a matter for subjective judgments within the limits described by relevant theory and subject matter expertise. The organization's control over these judgments does not extend far beyond its capacity for hiring able engineers, agronomists, economists, etc., who will come up with the best possible judgments consistent with the state of the arts. By contrast the aggregation procedures themselves can and should be exactly prescribed in order to transmit as far as possible and as correctly as possible all the information and judgments made on each of the relevant factors affecting the costs and benefits from a project.

Probability appraisal or risk analysis as discussed in Chapter III does nothing more than suggest that the proper probability calculus be used in aggregating probability judgments about the many events influencing the final outcome of a project. Just as it is generally accepted that $2 + 2$ is 4 and not 5, so there are logical, though less generally known, rules for aggregating probability distributions of uncertain events. A major reason why these rules have not been more widely used is the complexity and multitude of calculations which are required in their application. However, present-day availability of high-speed computers makes their application not only desirable but definitely feasible. The only exception to this recommendation is the case where even the most pessimistic estimates for *all* of the variables and parameters affecting a project's net benefits result in a satisfactory measure of the return.[8] In this case a probability appraisal might still satisfy some intellectual curiosity but would be redundant for the overall project decision. Even in this case, however, one could find it useful to do probability appraisals if the objective is to investigate alternative ways of implementing the project.

The primary purpose of Chapter III is to illustrate, with some highly stylized and hypothetical streams of costs and benefits, why application of the probability calculus to aggregation is important, and to show the sensitivity of the present value of a stream of net benefits to probability distributions and correlations of various basic events. The method of ap-

---

[8] Or conversely, where the most optimistic estimates result in an unsatisfactory return.

proximation by a simulated sample is briefly described, and recommended for estimation of probability distributions of rates of returns from actual projects. The simplicity of calculation and the adaptability of this method to any type of model and conceivable set of probability distributions make this a preferable method, provided that the resulting distribution is approximated by an adequate sample.[9] Only under very restrictive assumptions about the model and the distributions would it be practical to calculate means and standard deviations of an aggregated variable by using mathematical methods for aggregation. Mathematical aggregation of probability distributions may be useful also for partial analyses.

The final crucial phase of project appraisal is, of course, the ranking of alternative projects, or of courses of action to be taken in a given project. Unfortunately, precise recommendations can be made only on aggregate procedures. The choice on any alternative courses of action subject to uncertain outcomes, like the estimate of probability distributions, involves a large element of subjective judgment. A very large number of decisions cannot be classified in any objective way as "right" or "wrong" (in an a priori sense), no matter how utility or preferences are defined. Decisions involving public projects raise questions about the distribution of benefits and costs, and many differing preferences with respect to risk have to be taken into account. Some of these decision problems are discussed in Chapter IV. But while theory cannot suggest a unique general solution to these problems, it is nevertheless quite apparent that decision-makers *do* wish to know the likelihood of outcomes from alternative courses of action in order to reach decisions. Hence, project appraisals are better if they provide this information. Furthermore, there are certain limited activities of concern in project appraisal, such as gathering of additional information or strategies involving sequential decisions, which can be best appraised in a probabilistic decision framework. Chapter IV presents a brief discussion of the application of probabilistic information to such decision problems.

Practical procedures and problems in carrying out project evaluations which take account of uncertainty are reviewed in Part II. Any quantitative evaluation explicitly incorporating uncertainty requires construction of a mathematical model. In Chapter V it is demonstrated that preparation of a formal model does not require unusual mathematical skills. Several uses of such models, particularly when they are programmed for computerized calculations, are discussed. Illustrative applications of the methods discussed throughout the paper are presented in Chapters VI and VII.

---

[9] Probability appraisal by simulation is being applied to several IBRD projects. For case studies and tentative conclusions on methodological aspects, see Louis Pouliquen, *Risk Analysis in Project Appraisal*, a forthcoming World Bank Staff Occasional Paper.

II

ASSESSMENT OF UNCERTAIN EVENTS

Millions of dollars have been invested in Project A in anticipation of great benefits to the country. But on hindsight, the benefits have been disappointing or even inadequate to cover costs. Elsewhere, Project B has had far better results than anticipated during its planning stage. Should projects like Project A have never been undertaken and the Project B kind of investment have been expanded? This in a nutshell, is the problem which arouses interest in the study of decisions under uncertainty. Clearly, the success of one project and the failure of another is no evidence that a wrong decision has been made. They merely give rise to two kinds of questions: were the realized outcomes anticipated, or were they a complete surprise, and, given a "correct" anticipation, was the decision a "correct" one?[1]

Formulation of Anticipations

First, what is a "correct" anticipation? Does "correct" mean that an anticipation must be confirmed by the realization? Certainly not, if the anticipation in which we are interested is a single outcome.[2] It is almost

---

[1] The "optimal" decision problem is discussed in Chapter IV.

[2] If the outcomes of an event are observable many times over and if the decision pertains to the entire set of outcomes, an anticipation of a frequency distribution of outcomes might be *nearly* correct in the sense that an anticipation can be expected to be approximately realized (if the number of observations on which the anticipation is based and the number of realizations is large enough).

axiomatic that under uncertainty, no anticipation could be expected to be correct in this sense. Instead, a "correct" anticipation could be defined as one which is not refuted by a realization. Applying this criterion it is evident that a single valued anticipation of an outcome can hardly qualify. At the other extreme, an anticipation which stretches over the entire range of possible realizations will be a "correct" anticipation.

Unfortunately correct anticipations in this objective sense are not necessarily satisfactory for reaching decisions, and it is after all primarily for the purpose of making choices that anticipations are formulated. Correct anticipations in this sense are not even unique.

Consider for instance a statement of anticipation whereby an outcome is said to be highly likely within a given range and extremely unlikely outside this range. This anticipation is as "correct" as one which assigns no likelihoods at all to possible outcomes in the sense that no realizations could refute the stated anticipations. Similarly correct is a statement which assigns numerical values to the relative likelihoods of various outcomes— for instance a 60 percent likelihood that a certain crop yield will be between 80 and 100 and a 40 percent likelihood that the yield will be between 100 and 120. The choice between alternative formulations of correct anticipations must be sought then on other grounds.

Some seek to distinguish between good and bad formulations of the nature of uncertainty on the basis of relative *objectivity* in the derivation of the estimate. Clearly, a statement of anticipation which defines possible outcomes in terms of specific relative likelihoods is less universally acceptable than one which does not distinguish between likelihoods. Similarly, the likelihoods of outcomes of an event which can be observed many times over are less disputable than the likelihoods of a non-recurring event. It is not clear, however, how relevant an objective formulation of anticipations is for analyzing how investors do act or even ought to act.[3]

The Probabilistic Formulation

Most decision theories adopt a particular formulation of anticipations on the basis of how closely it is thought to correspond with the way decision-makers actually think about uncertain outcomes in relation to their deci-

---

[3] Game-theoretic decision models are primarily justified on the basis of their reliance on the objective formulation of anticipations. But then again it is difficult to see why the objective formulation of the uncertainty condition should be important when the choice criteria or the choice from among many decision models is a subjective matter.

sions.[4] There is pretty general agreement that the likelihoods of outcomes do concern decision-makers and that it makes little difference for a decision whether these likelihoods are judgments based on mere hunches or on an enormous amount of frequency evidence. Furthermore, since the likelihood of outcomes and, to a more limited extent, even the full range of outcomes generally cannot be objectively determined, it is now commonly accepted that "the uncertainty of the consequences, which is controlling for behaviour, is basically that existing in the mind of the chooser,"[5] that is, the evaluation of risk is subjective.

A Probabilistic Formulation Facilitates Aggregation

A good portion of this paper is devoted to an exposition of how investors and project appraisers might go about formulating their expectations about the outcomes from a given investment, say the rate of return or the discounted present value of net benefits. Any estimate of such an outcome from an investment usually needs to be developed from information about the effects of many variables (cost items, production quantities, prices, etc.) and their values. This is in essence what an investment appraisal is all about. Similarly, of course, the various outcomes from an investment under uncertainty conditions arise also from the wide range of values which relevant non-controllable variables and parameters of the relevant relationships take on as a result of uncertainty. Now, it may be satisfacotry (and "objectively" more correct than formulation of another anticipation) to say that production, prices and various cost items will fall into specified ranges. But, to "build" up an estimate of, say, the rate of return, from wide ranges of the relevant variables and parameters without regard to likelihoods, and particularly the likelihoods of compensating events, would lead to quite unacceptable results.

It is easy to see that there is little chance that all the worst, or the best,

---

[4] R. M. Aldeman, "Criteria for Capital Investment," *Operational Research Quarterly*, March 1965 summarizes the ongoing debate between objectivists and subjectivists pretty well: "As there are so many subjective elements in the choice of criterion to use, there seem to be no valid grounds for objecting to subjective elements within the criterion. Certainly, it seems that whenever a criterion containing subjective elements is proposed there will be cries that it is not objective. Likewise, however, if a criterion that claims objectivity is proposed, there are cries that it does not take into account the decision maker's subjective valuation of payoffs involved, nor his subjective beliefs."

[5] J. Marshak, "Alternative Approaches to the Theory of Choice in Risk-Taking Situations," *Econometrica*, Vol. 19, No. 4, October 1951, pp. 404–437.

of the anticipations will appear in combination. This is so no matter how difficult it is to specify the basic probability distributions. The only way, so far, to handle this aggregation problem is to use the probability calculus. It is one thing to believe that one event has as good a chance to turn out favorably as unfavorably, and another matter to believe that there is as much of a chance that luck or misfortune will hold out simultaneously for a large number of independent events as there is a chance for some turning out favorably and others unfavorably. If it is thought, for instance, that X, Y and Z are independent events (that is that their outcomes are in no way correlated), then the probability calculus tells us that the probability of encountering a combination of the most unfavorable outcomes of all three events is the product of the probabilities of the most unfavorable outcome of each event.[6]

To illustrate the aggregation effect we might consider a simple case. It is given in the context of choices faced by a decision-maker in the national interest rather than in the more usual context of an individual decision-maker. Let us suppose that a national planning organization is presented with a proposal for an investment which costs $1 million and which could yield a capitalized return of $10 million, but also could result in a complete failure, i.e. a loss of $1 million. It is quite conceivable that the director of the agency would then ask whether the chance of a $1 million loss is as high as 10 percent. Assuming the answer is yes, the decision of this particular director might be to reject the project. No further attempts at specifying more accurate probabilities would be needed.

Suppose now, however, that the same agency is presented with a proposal for five similar projects with the same cost and the same range of returns, and that the outcomes of these projects are not correlated, i.e. that the chance of failure of each project is independent of what happens to the other projects. The decision might now be extremely sensitive to the *probability* of a loss in each project because only if all five projects are losers will the investment package not yield a return equal to the cost of the five projects. If the chance of a complete failure for each project is only 10 percent, for instance, the chance he takes on getting no return on the investment package is only one in one hundred thousand. If chances for a complete failure of each project is 50 percent or 90 percent, respectively, the chance he takes on not recovering the investment cost of the package is 1/32 and 6/10, respectively. It is hard to conceive that these different probabilities will not matter for the planning director's decision. Plainly it

---

[6] If the most unfavorable outcomes are X_1, Y_1 and Z_1 and the respective probabilities are p_1, p_2 and p_3 then $p(X_1Y_1Z_1) = p_1 \cdot p_2 \cdot p_3$.

will be in his interest to find out. Note that this will be so whatever the risk aversion of the agency or its directors.[7]

A Probabilistic Approach Utilizes More Information

The appraisal and evaluation of a project is usually a collective effort of a team of experts. A good project appraisal draws on the knowledge of many disciplines such as engineering, agronomy, hydrology, statistics, economics, sociology, and politics. It is a major contention underlying the appraisal procedures suggested in this monograph that a good appraisal should attempt to distinguish between what each discipline and, if embodied within different individuals, what each expert contributes to the final appraisal and evaluation of a project. Particularly under uncertainty conditions these contributions tend to get confounded beyond recognition. It is then not uncommon for the agronomist or the engineer to "contribute" a production function which reflects his assessment of the political and social conditions or to "discount" the parameters by what he believes ought to be the government's attitudes towards particular outcomes. Conversely, and particularly if unaware that the engineer has already "colored" his estimate of technical coefficients, the person in charge of assessing a set of possible benefits from a project may "adjust" the technical coefficients to what he believes (and is in a best position to know) are "realistic" levels. There are, of course, many legitimate interaction effects which make it desirable and necessary for the different experts to collaborate in preparing projections. However, beyond these, projections of a particular event should as nearly as possible reflect what the appraiser believes to be the possible outcome of that event under explicitly stated conditions. This is in fact facilitated by the probabilistic approach.

When an engineer is required to summarize a projection of a particular event, say, the water yield supplied by a given size reservoir, in terms of one unique number, he must throw away a great deal of his knowledge about this event. Knowing that the unique estimate supplied by him will form the basis and the only basis for a unique estimate of a benefit-cost measure, he will be tempted to give an estimate which he believes to reflect the decision-maker's preference or aversion towards risk. He may give a most conservative estimate, one which he knows has a high probability to be exceeded; he may give what he believes to be the most likely outcome, or the mean of several outcomes, etc.

Conversely, the final decision-maker, who must consider the riskiness of

---

[7] Unless their risk aversion is 100 percent, in which case neither should be in business.

11

various projects in choosing between them, is in no less a difficult position. Deprived of knowledge of the likelihoods of realizing outcomes of some technical events other than those reported, he must estimate technical information which the engineer is in a better position to estimate and might have actually estimated but which due to faulty appraisal procedure has not been recorded.

A Probabilistic Formulation Can be Subjected to Meaningful Empirical Test

In our search for a good formulation of a statement of anticipation about an uncertain event, we have in essence rejected those formulations which either are practically always refuted by the actual outcome (the single valued estimate) or are never refuted (the range without probabilities). Note that a valuable attribute of the probability formulation is the fact that, while with it an anticipation cannot be refuted by a single outcome of an event, it can be so refuted at least in a probability sense by observing several outcomes of an event. In a sense then one could say that in a world of uncertainty the only correct and useful knowledge and information is that which is reported in probability terms and can be refuted in these terms.

Estimation of Probability Distributions

Few cut-and-dried rules can be given for actually estimating the probability distributions of basic events or parameters used in a cost-benefit analysis. Very often it might mean nothing more than stating explicitly the information experts have been using all along in making their projections. For instance, if annual rainfall is one of the uncertain variables, a frequency distribution derived from past observations may be available and used if meteorologists think that this is the best estimate of the probability distribution of future rainfall. Frequently it is thought that a better estimate of the probability distribution could be obtained by fitting the frequency data to a known curve.

Estimates of parameters such as price and income elasticities or production coefficients are often derived by formal statistical analyses of data. Probability distributions of the parameters could often be derived from the same data.

If a formal statistical distribution is either not available to provide a "best estimate," or if available is inappropriate, the expert has to use less sophisticated methods to obtain a profile of the distribution of an event. He may proceed by first projecting the limits of the range of possible outcomes on the basis of historical or other comparable data, and/or of his experience with the event under similar circumstances. This range can

12

then be subdivided into two to five subranges, ranked on the basis of "more" or "less likely." Subsequently relative magnitudes can be assigned to these ranges, such that the sum of the weights add up to unity. Alternatively, it may be easier sometimes to ask for the limits of the range which encompasses the actual outcome of a certain event *with a specified probability*.

Depending on the variable involved and on how one wishes to use the probability information, it may be desirable to specify a continuous distribution or one which is specified for discrete values of a variable. Often one may be satisfied with estimating the range which encompasses all or almost all likely outcomes and then to assume on the basis of prior knowledge that the variable is distributed as one of several known theoretical probability distributions. If a normal distribution is hypothesized for instance, it is sufficient to ask for what the "expert" believes to be the mean or the mode and the limits of the range which would have a rare chance of being exceeded. If a Beta distribution is hypothesized, the mean and standard deviation can be estimated by asking the expert for a pessimistic (p), most likely (m) and optimistic (o) prediction.[8]

The main point to be stressed with regard to the assessment of probability distributions of basic events and parameters affecting the returns of a project is that it is desirable to avoid "coloring" these probability judgments by risk preference or risk aversion considerations. The estimated probability distribution should as nearly as possible reflect what the appraiser believes to be the possible outcomes of a particular event and their respective likelihoods. A project may be rejected because it may have a small chance of failure, regardless of a high probability of success, but this does not at all imply that it is appropriate to neglect reporting of probabilities for highly favorable outcomes of basic events (such as physical yields and prices). The reason for this and the inappropriateness of appraising only limited aspects of the probability distributions will be explained later on.

Estimation of probability distribution is simply a way of stating explicitly, as best we know how, what we do know about the outcome of a particular event. Thus a probability distribution estimate is avowedly subjective and its foresight is limited. However, it is difficult to see how, except by mere chance, *ignoring* whatever little is or can be known about an event, can possibly result in a more useful appraisal.

---

[8] The mean is then $(p + o + 4m)/6$ and the standard deviation is $(o - p)/6$. For a good discussion of estimating probability distributions in the context of investment appraisal, see B. Wagle, "A Statistical Analysis of Risk in Capital Investment Projects," *Operations Research Quarterly*, Vol. 18, No. 1.

III

PROBABILITY APPRAISAL OF
PROJECT RETURNS
UNDER UNCERTAINTY

General Outline

Project appraisal in general involves an evaluation of how certain simple events interact to produce a final outcome. Assuming certainty about the state of the simple events and the relationship between them and a final outcome, the appraisal of an investment consists essentially of identifying the events most relevant to the final outcome of a given course of action, such as the outputs A, B, C . . . ., the required inputs D, C, E . . . ., and the corresponding prices. Subsequently, logical (mathematically correct) procedures such as addition and multiplication are used to calculate the economic returns of the project.

An adequate appraisal of projects involving uncertainty requires judgments, exactly as under certainty, of the kind of events relevant to the outcome from a given course of action. But instead of presenting exact estimates of the relevant events, an appraiser must form a judgment of the likelihoods of various states of the same events. He must then use the probability calculus to derive meaningful aggregations of the interactions of the simple events. This chapter primarily deals with reasonably correct aggregation procedures for deriving a probability distribution of a cost-benefit measure used in project appraisal. Concern here is with the logical steps to be taken in aggregating probability beliefs of investment appraisers about various relatively "simple" events into probability distributions of the total net benefits from an investment. Correct aggregation procedures do not, of course, in any way substitute for "good" judgments in the choice of relevant variables and their estimated projected probability distributions. They are merely a means for assuring that "good" judgments are preserved in the process of aggregation.

The Aggregation Problem

It will be useful here to review briefly the benefit-cost calculations used most commonly in investment appraisals, when uncertainty is not explicitly taken into consideration. This review and somewhat formal and precise way of stating the commonly used procedures will assist us, however, in learning the modifications needed in any analysis which explicitly takes account of uncertainty about the outcomes of specified elements in the analysis. The basic benefit-cost formula is:

$$R = \sum (1 + r)^{-t} B_t \qquad t = 0, 1, \ldots, n \qquad (1)$$

where R is the total net benefit from an investment discounted to the present time t, B_t is the annual *net* benefit and r is the marginal cost of capital.[1]

The estimates of annual benefits and costs are, of course, derived from knowledge about certain other variables. Even in the crudest form of analysis, the appraiser would have to consider various changes in the production of goods and services, their respective values and the quantities and costs of the resources needed as a result of the investment. In a more comprehensive appraisal, further explicitly stated relationships may be used to estimate the net benefits. Prices, for instance, may be related to projected per capita incomes, population, imports or exports. In case of an irrigation project, additional outputs may be a function of moisture deficiency or rainfall, and the number of producing units affected by the investment may depend on the available amount of water (which in turn depends on rainfall) and the farmers' responsiveness to adopt new methods of farming.

In a very general way, the total net benefits from an investment can be said to be a function of some exogenous variables and parameters which describe the quantitative relationship between variables. Exogenous vari-

---

[1] A variant of this formula is the internal rate of return calculation, in which case r is calculated from formula (1), letting R equal zero; then r (the internal rate of return) is compared to the cost of capital. For the exposition intended in this chapter, it makes no difference whether R or r is the final variable which is sought.

ables are variables which an analyst chooses not to explain in any formal way by other functional relationships, either because the state of the variable has only a small effect on the variable which is of interest, or because he finds it too difficult, time-consuming and costly to carry out further analysis, or finally because the variables which explain are as difficult to forecast as the variable to be explained. For instance, the analyst may choose not to explain the price of fertilizer because this variable has only a small effect on the net benefits for a certain irrigation project. On the other hand, he may not choose to study the prices of products in any formal way because price forecasting is a costly and time-consuming activity. Finally, he may choose not to study the functional relationship between yields and rainfall because he cannot forecast rainfall in the future any better than he can directly forecast yields.

The problem which concerns us in this chapter is how to aggregate probability distributions of exogenous variables and parameters. For an oversimplified illustration, consider a simple project whose costs and benefits are fully realized in two years, such that the present value R is,

$$R = aB_1 + a^2B_2 \tag{2}$$

where $a = (1 + r)^{-1}$, r is the opportunity cost of capital, B_1 is the net return (positive or negative) in the first year and B_2 is the net return in the second year. Assume furthermore that B_1 is the sum of two costs which in turn are the products of physical inputs and their unit costs, Y_1 and Y_2 and C_1 and C_2 respectively. B_2 is the sum of net revenues derived from two sources which in turn are the products of physical outputs and their per unit prices, X_1 and X_2 and V_1 and V_2 respectively, i.e.

$$B_1 = C_1\,Y_1 + C_2\,Y_2 \tag{3}$$

and

$$B_2 = V_1\,X_1 + V_2\,X_2 \tag{4}$$

Furthermore, physical output X_2 is known to be a quadratic function of a certain input Z. The parameters of this functional relationship are also random variables subject to probability distributions, i.e.

$$X_2 = e_0 + e_1\,Z + e_2\,Z^2 \tag{5}$$

Then, by substituting equations (3), (4) and (5) into (2), the present value can be seen to be a function of the exogenous variables C_1, C_2, Y_1, Y_2, P_1, P_2, X_1 and Z and the parameters a, e_0, e_1 and e_2:

$$R = a(C_1\,Y_1 + C_2\,Y_2) + a^2(V_1\,X_1 + V_2\,e_0 + V_2\,e_1\,Z + V_2\,e_2\,Z^2) \tag{6}$$

One procedure for deriving the probability distributions of R is to recompute equation (6) for each possible combination of the outcomes of the basic variables, and furthermore, to calculate the probability of each combination. Assuming that the probability distribution of each variable is stated in terms of four possible outcomes, even such a crude and simple analysis as described here would require $(4)^{11} = 4{,}194{,}304$ calculations, 11 being the number of basic variables. In the analysis of an actual project with benefits stretching out over many years, the number of variables would be much higher, and in spite of possible shortcuts and even higher calculating speeds of electronic computers, it is difficult to see that this procedure has any great merit. Recall that in addition to calculating the returns, the computer would need to calculate also the product of all the probabilities for each combination and then to reaggregate the returns and their probabilities into a distribution.

A second procedure which is certainly feasible is to estimate the probability distribution of R on the basis of a *simulated sample*.[2] All possible outcomes of the variables affecting the returns from a project and their probabilities are fed into a computer. The computer is then instructed to select at random one outcome of each of the variables, allowing for realistic restrictions for interdependencies in the variables. Given the selected outcomes of all the variables, the corresponding net present returns of the investment are calculated. This process is repeated until a large enough sample is obtained for a close approximation to the actual probability distribution of the returns (R). This procedure requires absolutely no new mathematical skills on the part of project appraisers. They merely must supply estimates of probability distributions. There are already available computer programs which (a) select at random values from these distributions, (b) calculate the present value or internal rate of return or any other measure of project benefits and (c) after repeating the same process a desired number of times compute a frequency distribution of the measure of benefits. In practice, the size of the sample is determined by trial and error. The sample is considered large enough when the frequency distribution does not change much when the sample size is further increased.

A third procedure is to apply the probability calculus directly to the calculation of certain characteristics of the probability distribution of R (or any other measure of aggregated benefits). This procedure is based on the application of one of the most important concepts involving probability distributions, namely, that of mathematical expectations. In the next two

---

[2] This method is sometimes referred to as *stochastic simulation*. A remarkably lucid exposition of the method is given by D. B. Hertz, "Risk Analysis in Capital Expenditure Decisions," *Harvard Business Review*, January/February, 1964.

17

sections we will discuss the limitations as well as the attractive features of the two practically feasible aggregation procedures—the simulation method and the mathematical method—by illustrations.

Illustration of Alternative Procedures for Aggregating Probability Distributions

At this point a very simple illustration of what has been discussed so far should be useful. While it is usually not feasible to calculate the exact probability distribution of an aggregate measure (the first procedure outlined above), a very simple case is presented here in which an exact distribution can be easily calculated. Subsequently, the two approximation procedures will be used and the results compared with the "true" distribution.

The object is to know the probability distribution of a present value of net revenue (R), based on knowledge of the probability distributions of an initial investment cost (Y) and a revenue (X), discounted by a factor of 0.5 (say the revenue is received ten years later and the discount rate is 7 percent), thus

(Present Value) = (.5)(Gross Revenue) − (Investment Cost),

or in symbols

$$R = (.5)(X) - Y \qquad (7)$$

The assumed probability distribution of X and Y are given in Table 1.

TABLE 1: Probability Distributions of Revenue (X) and Investment Cost (Y)

X (Revenue)		Y (Investment Cost)	
Value	Probability	Value	Probability
20	.10	8	.20
22	.20	10	.60
25	.40	12	.20
28	.20		
30	.10		

The "true" distribution of the present value is derived by calculating R for each possible combination of X and Y, and the probability of each combination to occur. In this case there are 15 possible combinations. Assuming that the distribution of X and Y are independent (i.e. that the probabilities of getting a particular value of X are in no way affected by what value of Y has occurred or vice versa), the probability of any particular combination of X and Y is the product of the probabilities of the respective values of X and Y. For instance, the probability of X having a value

18

of 20 and Y a value of 8 is $(.10)(.20) = .02$. The true probability distribution of R based on the assumed probability distributions of X and Y given in Table 1 is presented in the second column of Table 2.

TABLE 2: Probability Distributions of Present Value (R)

Present Value (R)	"True" Distribution	Simulated Sample (50 observations)	Simulated Sample (100 observations)
		Probabilities	
−2	.02	.06	.03
−1	.04	0	.03
0	.06	.04	.05
0.5	.08	.06	.07
1	.12	.08	.06
2	.06	.06	.08
2.5	.24	.30	.21
3	.06	.02	.03
4	.12	.14	.15
4.5	.08	.10	.13
5	.06	.04	.03
6	.04	.10	.10
7	.02	0	.03
Mean:	2.50	2.77	2.94
Variance:	3.75	3.82	4.24

To estimate the probability distribution of R by *simulation*, it is necessary to draw at random a large number of X and Y values from their respective probability distributions and to compute a value of R for each set of X and Y values drawn. The frequency distribution of R when a large enough sample is used will tend to approximate the "true" probability distribution of R. (In the case used for illustration, there would be no point, of course, to use the simulated sampling method, since the total number of possible combinations is only 15, while a "large enough" sample would require a minimum of, say, 100 "observations" on R.)

To illustrate the method of simulation by a sample, we have used the last digits of telephone numbers in a directory as a randomization device.[3] Samples of size 50 and 100 were chosen by drawing the appropriate number of observations for each X and Y and pairing them at random. To obtain the values of X, for instance, we let the last digit (0) represent an X value of 20, (1) and (2) a value of 22, (3), (4), (5) and (6) a value of 25, (7) and (8) a value of 28 and (9) a value of 30. To obtain a series of Y numbers, we

---

[3] There exist many random selection computer "packages" which select at random values from various kinds of probability distributions.

let a last digit of (0) and (1) represent a Y value of 8, (2), (3), (4), (5), (6) and (7) a value of 10 and (8) and (9) a value of 12. The probability distributions of R corresponding with 50 and 100 pairs of randomly selected X and Y values from their respective probability distributions are presented in Columns 3 and 4 of Table 2.

The third procedure consists of calculating the mean and the variance of the present value (R) and interpreting the results in terms of a *normal distribution*. This is, of course, only an approximation procedure, since we know already that in our case, the "true" distribution is a discrete distribution (i.e. the variables in which we are interested take on only discrete values) and the probabilities do not follow an exact pattern as would be expected from a normal distribution. To begin with, however, let us see how to calculate the mean and the variance of R and how to interpret these in terms of a normal distribution.

Denote the means of X and Y by $\bar{X}$ and $\bar{Y}$ respectively, and their variances by $V(X)$ and $V(Y)$. In our case, (from the basic data presented in Table 1):

$$\bar{X} = \sum (\text{probability of an event } i)(X_i)$$
$$= (.10)\,(20) + (.20)\,(22) + (.40)\,(25) + (.20)\,(28) + (.10)\,(30) = 25$$
$$\bar{Y} = \sum (\text{prob } i)\,(Y_i)$$
$$= (.20)\,(8) + (.60)\,(10) + (.20)\,(12) = 10$$
$$V(X) = \sum (\text{prob } i)\,(X_i - \bar{X})^2$$
$$= (.10)\,(-5)^2 + (.20)\,(-3)^2 + .20\,(3)^2 + .10\,(5)^2 = 8.6$$

and

$$V(Y) = \sum (\text{prob } i)\,(Y_i - \bar{Y})^2$$
$$= .20\,(-2)^2 + .20\,(2)^2 = 1.6$$

Given these data, it is a simple matter to calculate the mean, $\bar{R}$, and the variance, $V(R)$, of the present value as follows (it will be recalled that the revenue is discounted to present value by a factor of .5):

$$R = (.5)\,(\bar{X}) - \bar{Y}$$
$$= (.5)\,(25) - 10 = 2.5$$

and

$$V(R) = (.5)^2\,V(X) + V(Y)$$
$$= (.25)\,(8.6) + (1.6) = 3.75$$

assuming that X and Y are not correlated.[4]

---

[4] See Annex for the mathematical derivation of the formulae. Note that the mean and variance calculated by these formulae are the "true" mean and variance of R.

To determine the probability that R is less than any value, R_i, one computes the ratio $\dfrac{(R_i - R)}{\sqrt{V(R)}}$ and looks up the probability in a table of the standard normal distribution. The cumulative distribution based on the assumption that R approximates a normal distribution is given in the last column of Table 3, and is presented graphically in Figure 1. For comparison, the cumulative probabilities from the "true" probability distribution and the simulated samples are also presented in Table 3 and Figure 1. A cumulative distribution shows the probabilities that the event will be less than a stated value.

TABLE 3: Cumulative Probability Distribution of R

Cumulative Probabilities, Prob. $(R < R_i)$

Present Value R_i	"True" Distribution	Sample 50 Observations	Sample 100 Observations	Approximation by Normal Distribution
−2.0	0.02	0.06	0.03	0.01
−1.0	0.06	0.06	0.06	0.04
0	0.12	0.10	0.11	0.10
0.5	0.20	0.16	0.18	0.15
1.0	0.32	0.24	0.24	0.22
2.0	0.38	0.30	0.32	0.40
2.5	0.62	0.60	0.53	0.50
3.0	0.68	0.62	0.56	0.60
4.0	0.80	0.76	0.71	0.78
4.5	0.88	0.80	0.84	0.85
5.0	0.94	0.90	0.87	0.90
6.0	0.98	1.00	0.97	0.96
7.0	1.00	1.00	1.00	0.99

Discussion of Alternative Estimating Procedures

The brief illustration and comparison of results of the two estimation procedures—the simulation method and the mathematical method—suffices to point up, at least in principle, the possible advantageous features and the shortcomings of both methods.

For simulation the project appraiser needs no knowledge of the probability calculus whatsoever. There is no chance of making any error in the calculations. All the appraiser needs to do is to present the computer with a model and the constant values or probability distributions of the relevant parameters and variables, and the computer (with a programmer's aid) can grind out an estimated probability distribution of the desired aggregate measure. Furthermore, this method requires no assumptions with respect to the relevant final distributions, since the calculated sample gives directly an estimate of the "true" distribution, whatever its shape.

FIGURE 1

CUMULATIVE PROBABILITY DISTRIBUTIONS OF PRESENT VALUE

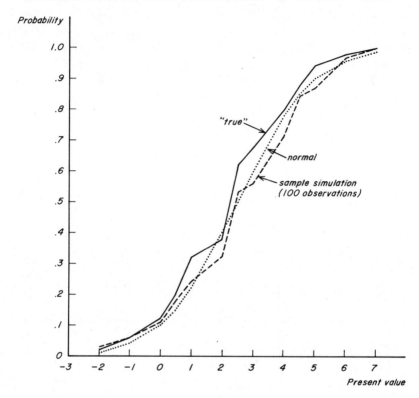

The primary disadvantage of the simulation method is its complete reliance on the availability of a computer. Furthermore, any "run" is highly specific to the postulated inputs. If any variations in the assumptions or in the project itself are to be investigated, a new computer "run" is necessary. Frequently, while still in the field, an appraisal team may wish to pursue consideration of alternatives based on the results of a previous analysis. With simulation this may not be feasible. Another unresolved issue is the optimum sample size. However, since in most cases very little computing time on a large computer will be required, the practical solution might be to choose a relatively large sample, or to devise a sampling procedure by stages with a statistical test to determine whether additional observations should be calculated. In this case, the variance would be estimated from an initial sample. This in conjunction with preassigned confidence intervals can be used to determine the adequate sample size.

22

The mathematical method is only useful if one wishes to consider a relatively simple model consisting of aggregation of only a few major uncertain variables. In this case, the method is cheap, requiring little more than pencil and paper and a desk calculator. Furthermore, once the mean and the variance have been calculated for one set of parameters, it is easy to estimate the effects of changes in any of the parameters or probability distributions of the important variables on the mean and variance of the desired aggregate measure.

The mathematical method does require some minimal knowledge of the probability calculus; however, this is no major problem. An investment appraiser usually knows how to calculate means and variances and can be easily familiarized with a few basic rules needed for deriving the mean and variance of an aggregative measure.[5] The real problem is to determine how useful it is to know the mean and the variance if one does not know the exact shape of the probability distribution of the aggregate measure.

There are several ways of "sweeping the distribution problem under the table." None, however, are completely satisfactory. There are, for instance, some decision-makers, or so it is assumed in much of the literature on risk appraisal, whose objective function is such that they require to know only the mean and variance. This aspect of the problem is further discussed in the following chapter. At least very superficially, however, it may be seriously questioned whether decision-making under uncertainty can be generally reduced to a maximization of a weighted function of a mean and variance of some measure of income. On the other hand, particularly when one wishes to consider various alternative ways of designing a given project which will be subject therefore, to essentially the same kind of probability distribution, it may be quite sufficient to have information on the means and variances of alternative designs.

Then there are, of course, quite a number of projects for which the aggregate measure of the net benefits would be approximately characterized by a normal distribution, which is completely specified once the mean and variance are known. Say, for instance, that the present value is simply the sum of a string of discounted annual net benefits, each of which are assumed to follow a normal distribution. In this case, the present value would indeed be a normal distribution as well.[6] Furthermore, even if the annual net benefits were not normally distributed, the present value distribution would still be approximately normal, if a large number of annual benefits with approximately equal weights were to be summed (i.e. if the interest

---

[5] Some of these basic rules are given in the Annex.

[6] The internal rate of return, however, would not be exactly normally distributed.

rate were relatively low).[7] There is no assurance, however, that the interpretation of the calculated mean and variance of a present value of an internal rate of return in terms of a normal probability distribution is a reasonable procedure in all cases. It is first of all an empirical question how much the true distribution deviates from normality; also it depends how sensitive the decision criteria are.

The data presented in Table 3 illustrates the problem fairly well. The true distribution of the aggregate measure R is certainly not a normal distribution, yet the cumulative probabilities estimated by using the mathematical expectations method and interpreting the mean and variance in terms of a normal distribution do not differ much from the "true" cumulative probabilities. Certainly, the distribution derived from a sample of 100 does not give better estimates (though a sufficiently large sample would have had at least a high probability of doing better).

In summary, as a matter of general practice the simulation method is the preferable method whenever a complete probability appraisal is desired. With computers becoming increasingly accessible and appropriate programs more generally available, the simulation method is likely to be actually less costly both in terms of manpower and mathematical skills required than the mathematical method. In addition and quite importantly, simulation is likely to give a better estimate of the true distribution than can be expected from assuming a normal distribution. The mathematical method is likely to prove useful, however, if partial analysis of the impact of uncertainty in a few selected variables is desired and quick approximate answers are needed.

For the remainder of this chapter only the mathematical appraisal method is used in order (a) to show how, in general, the results from a probability appraisal may differ from the results obtained by a conventionally practiced project appraisal, and (b) in order to illustrate further some essential rules from the probability calculus. The simulation procedure is not very well suited for deriving generalizations and is simple and straightforward enough not to require further illustrations.[8]

Conceptual Problems Related to Probability Appraisal

Throughout the discussion so far we have assumed that the reason for making a probability appraisal is that decision-makers are interested in knowing not merely a single-valued measure of a project's outcome, such

---

[7] This is shown by the Central Limit Theorem.

[8] See, however, Chapter VI.

24

as the one most likely or an average, but also other possible outcomes and their respective probabilities. Under the heading of "Biased estimates" below we explain why probability appraisal is desirable even if the decision-maker were to be satisfied with merely knowing a single valued estimate. Another problem discussed in this section is the problem of estimating the probability distribution of the present value or the internal rate of return for stochastic variables, some of which are correlated.

Biased estimates

Even if the decision-maker were interested only in a single point estimate and not in the entire probability distribution, it would be desirable to do a probability appraisal in some cases in order to avoid consistent errors of estimation.

One example is the practice of aggregating most likely values (modes) of various variables. To illustrate the folly of this method of aggregation, consider first a simple case where one is interested in estimating the most likely revenue from forecasts of price and sales. Say the market analyst predicts a 60 percent chance that the price will be $10 and a 40 percent chance that the price will be only $5. Sales are given a 60 percent chance to be 100 units and a 40 percent chance to be 50 units. The most likely revenue calculated from the most likely price and most likely sales is obviously $1,000. However, a probability appraisal would have clearly shown that this is not the correct estimate of the most likely revenue. Assuming that price and sales are not correlated, the true probability distribution of revenue is as follows:

Price	Sales	Probability	Revenue
10	10	.36	1,000
10	5	.24	500
5	10	.24	500
5	5	.16	250

Clearly, the most likely revenue is $500 (with a probability of .48) and not $1,000 (with a probability of .36). In general, when an aggregate measure is the (weighted) sum of many different variables or products of variables, the simple aggregation of modes will not give an accurate estimate of the true mode of the aggregate measure.

The same reasoning, of course, applies when one is interested in getting a "conservative" estimate, where such an estimate is defined as an outcome which has a large chance of being exceeded. If one were to aggregate such conservative estimates for different prices and sales, etc., the result would generally be a rate of return with an undefined extent of "conservativeness." In fact, to follow such a rule-of-thumb would certainly lead to non-comparable rates of returns estimates for different projects in terms of the degree of "conservatism" implied.

The problem of bias exists also if one is aggregating means of probability distributions of several elementary events to estimate a mean of the aggregate. Fortunately, there are likely to be many cases when such estimates are not biased, however. One such case is if the aggregate is a function linear in the uncertain variables. Say present value (R) is a sum of the discounted benefits (B) in several years. Then the mean of revenue ($\bar{R}$) is the sum of the discounted mean annual benefits ($\bar{B}$), i.e.

$$\bar{R} = \bar{B}_0 + a\bar{B}_1 + a^2\bar{B}_2 + \ldots\ldots\ldots \tag{8}$$

where $a = (1 + r)^{-1}$ and r is the discount rate.

But there are many cases when the dependent variable is a function which is non-linear in the independent variable. Consider, for instance, that one wishes to estimate the mean yield ($\bar{Y}$) of an agricultural crop based on one's knowledge about rainfall (W) and yield (Y) and the probability distribution of rainfall. Assume, furthermore, that yield (Y) increases at a decreasing rate when rainfall (W) increases in a given range, such that

$$Y = 10 + 6\,W - 0.5\,W^2 \tag{9}$$

Assume that W has a 50 percent chance of being 1 and 50 percent chance of being 5. Correspondingly, the yield has equal chances of being 15.5 and 27.5 and the true mean yield is 21.5. If, however, instead of a complete probability appraisal we had calculated the mean yield by substituting the mean rainfall ($\bar{W} = 3$) in the last equation our estimate would have been 23.5. This overestimate is, of course, intuitively expected since a decreasing rate in yield additions implies that a loss in yield due to a less than average rainfall is not fully compensated by the gain in yield when rainfall is more than average to the same extent. The notion of bias can be seen very easily, graphically, at least in this simple example. In Figure 2, $\bar{Y}$ is the "true" expected yield, whereas $f(\bar{W})$ is the estimate which would be obtained by simply substituting $\bar{W}$ for W in the yield equation.

Since non-linear functions used in economic projections are frequently convex (increasing at a decreasing rate), the likely bias from neglecting to do a proper probability analysis is likely to be an overestimation of benefits. For instance, if we base an estimate of benefits from irrigation on average water availability we are likely to overestimate the benefits if water availability is highly variable and the additional returns to water beyond

26

FIGURE 2
ILLUSTRATION OF BIAS WHEN YIELD IS CALCULATED AS A
FUNCTION OF AVERAGE RAINFALL

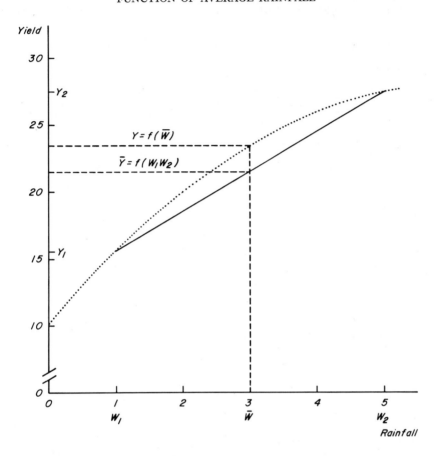

the average amount are small in comparison with the loss in revenue due to an amount of water less than the average. A likely source of a similar bias in project appraisal is the calculation of cost-benefits on the basis of an average life of the investment. The present value as a function of investment life certainly increases at a decreasing rate. Thus there is a possibility of bias similar to that shown in Figure 2, if for instance there is held to be an equal possibility of the life being 10 years or 50 years. The bias can be quite large, particularly if the discount rate is high and the average investment life fairly short. Several possible sources of such biases are discussed below. The point to be made is that it may be desirable to do a complete

27

probability appraisal even if the appraiser is only interested in a single-valued estimate and not in the entire probability distribution of some measure of a project's benefits.

Correlation

A major problem in appraising a project subject to stochastic events is correlation. Generally, the existence of correlation indicates incomplete model specification. Therefore, if significant correlations are suspected, the best way to avoid misleading predictions is explicitly to recognize further underlying systematic relationships among variables and to substitute uncorrelated variables. The problem of correlation and how to cope with it can be best illustrated by a few examples.

Consider that the objective is to estimate revenue (R) based on prior estimates of price (T) and sales (S), i.e.

$$R = (T)(S) \tag{10}$$

Assume, furthermore, that the price is believed to have a 50–50 chance of being 1 or 3 and similarly sales have a 50–50 chance of being 200 or 400. The distribution, mean and variance of the revenue, assuming no correlation, are as follows:

Probability	Combination (Price, Sales)	Revenue (R)	Mean and Variance
.25	(1,200)	200	$\bar{R} = 600$
.25	(1,400)	400	$V(R) = 140,000$
.25	(3,200)	600	
.25	(3,400)	1,200	

By contrast, if price and sales in the above example had been perfectly correlated, if for instance, whenever sales are 200, price is 3, and whenever sales are 600, price is 1, then the "true" distribution of revenue, the mean and variance would have been as follows:

Probability	Combination (Price, Sales)	Revenue (R)	Mean and Variance
.50	1,400	400	$\bar{R} = 500$
.50	3,200	600	$V(R) = 10,000$

Clearly, whether or not price and sales are correlated makes quite a

28

difference in how we should calculate the distribution of revenue. Both mean and variance of the product of price and sales are different, depending on the extent of correlation. The correlation between price and sales could have been accounted for by specifying an additional equation describing the relationship between sales and price as follows:

$$T = 5 - .01\ S \qquad (11)$$

or if price and sales are not perfectly correlated as implied by the linear demand function (11), then by

$$T = 5 - .01\ S + e \qquad (12)$$

where e represents random effects on price not correlated with sales. The mathematical equations for deriving the mean and variance of the revenue in both the correlated and uncorrelated case are presented in the Annex.

Another likely source of correlation is that two or more variables are related in a systematic way to a third variable. For illustration, consider that we wish to calculate the probability distribution of a total revenue on the basis of what we believe are the probability distributions of revenue from two sources, R_1 and R_2, i.e.

$$R = R_1 + R_2 \qquad (13)$$

given the following data:

Probability	Revenue (1) R_1	Probability	Revenue (2) R_2
.50	50	.50	40
.50	90	.50	60

and disregarding the possibility of correlation, the probability distribution of total revenue, its mean and variance are summarized below:

Probability	Combination $[R_1,\ R_2]$		Total Revenue (R)	Mean and Variance
.25	50,	40	90	$\bar{R} = 120$
.25	50,	60	110	$V(R) = 500$
.25	90,	40	130	
.25	90,	60	150	

If, however, the uncertainty in both revenues had the same underlying cause (say both would be the higher of the given values if a protective

29

tariff were to prevail and enactment of the legislation were given a 50–50 chance), then R_1 and R_2 are perfectly correlated. The corresponding probability distribution mean and variance of total revenue would in this case be as follows:

Probability	Combination $[R_1, \quad R_2]$	Revenue (R)	Mean and Variance
.50	(50, 40)	90	$\bar{R} = 120$
.50	(90, 60)	150	$V(R) = 900$

Note that correlation does not affect the mean of a sum. However, the variance can be substantially altered by the presence of correlation. Further specification of the model would have given an explicit equation for the close relationship of the respective revenues with the size of tariff (Z). From our data we can interpolate that these relationships may be as follows:

$$R_1 = 50 + 4Z \tag{14}$$

and

$$R_2 = 40 + 2Z \tag{15}$$

Adding these equations to the model we would substitute (14) and (15) into (13), i.e.

$$R = 90 + 6Z \tag{16}$$

and estimate the probability distribution of total revenue, its mean and variance directly from this equation, as follows:

Probability	Tariff (Z)	Total Revenue	Mean and Variance
.50	0	90	$\bar{R} = 120$
.50	1.0	150	$V(R) = 900$

It should be recalled, as noted earlier, that the method of calculating all possible outcomes is not an operational procedure and is used here only to illustrate concepts. In the next section we will show how to estimate the mean and variance of total revenue by using the mathematics of expectations.[9]

---

[9] The mean and variance can be readily calculated from equation (16). Note that $\bar{Z} = 5$ and $V(Z) = 25$. Then $\bar{R} = 90 + 6(5) = 120$ and $V(R) = (6^2)(25) = 900$.

The problem of correlation, then, is the problem of accounting for relationships between the included variables themselves, and between included variables and excluded variables. Since in any practical appraisal only a few relationships can be explicitly stated, one could not possibly hope for the removal of all correlation. The best one can hope for is that the problem is recognized and understood, and that the appraiser explicitly accounts for the more important relationships and makes judgments about their quantitative nature.

Specific Uncertainty Problems in Project Appraisal

The purpose of the ensuing discussion is twofold: to illustrate how to calculate the mean and variance of the present value and other selected variables and to derive some generalizations for assessing projects subject to uncertainty. The operational uses of the mathematical estimation procedure are, of course, limited to highly stylized appraisal models. These, however, are often quite useful at least as preliminary exercises prior to a more complete appraisal.

Uncertainty about annual net benefits

Let us begin by assuming that the appraisal has proceeded to the point of having an estimate of a stream of annual benefits (positive or negative), that the annual benefits can be estimated in terms of probability distributions and that the discount rate is known. The expected (mean) present value ($\bar{R}$) is then simply a weighted sum of the expected (mean) annual benefits, i.e.

$$\bar{R} = \bar{B}_0 + a\bar{B}_1 + a^2\bar{B}_2 + \ldots. \tag{17}$$

where $a = (1 + r)^{-1}$ and r is the discount rate. Note that for estimating the mean present value it matters not whether successive benefits are correlated. The variance of R, $V(R)$, depends very much on the extent of correlation between successive benefits. If successive benefits are not correlated the variance of the present value is

$$V(R) = V(B_0) + a^2 V(B_1) + a^4 V(B_2) + \ldots + a^{2t} V(B_t) \ldots. \tag{18}$$

But, if the benefits are perfectly correlated,

$$V(R) = [\sqrt{V(B_0)} + a\sqrt{V(B_1)} + a^2\sqrt{V(B_2)}$$
$$+ \ldots + a^t\sqrt{V(B_t)} + \ldots]^2 \tag{19}$$

31

Equal annual correlated and uncorrelated benefits

The above equations for deriving the mean and variance of the present value can be easily solved when a large number of successive benefits have means and variances which are equal or follow a general trend. Let us first assume that annual benefits consist of a known or unknown level of benefits, B, and positive or negative, but from year to year uncorrelated deviations from this level, e_t, such that,

$$B_t = B + e_t \qquad (20)$$

Then, if B is known and e_t is assumed to be zero on the average, $\bar{B}_t = B$ and $V(B_t) = V(e)$. Since we have assumed that the e_t in successive years are not correlated, the annual benefits are clearly not correlated as well. If B, the level of the annual benefits, is not known except in terms of an average $\bar{B}$ and a variance $V(B)$, but e_t is zero in all years, $\bar{B}_t = \bar{B}$ and $V(B_t) = V(B)$. In this case the annual benefits are perfectly correlated. We now proceed to analyze the corresponding calculations of the mean and variance of the present value of a stream of benefits in these two extreme cases.

Regardless of whether successive benefits are correlated, the mean of the present value is

$$\bar{R} = \left(\sum a^t\right) \bar{B} \qquad (21)$$

where a is $(1 + r)^{-1}$ and r is the discount rate. However, the variance of the present value depends on correlation.[10] If the successive benefits are uncorrelated, i.e. if the uncertainty is due to year to year fluctuations,

$$V(R) = \left(\sum a^{2t}\right) V(e_t) \qquad (22)$$

If the level of benefits is the only source of uncertainty,

$$V(R) = \left(\sum a^t\right)^2 V(B) \qquad (23)$$

Derivation of these equations is discussed in the Annex. Values of $\left(\sum a^{2t}\right)$ for up to 30 years and 6 percent and 10 percent discount rates are presented in Annex Table 1.

As should be expected, the variance in the present value is relatively much smaller when successive benefits are uncorrelated than when they are positively correlated. For instance, we may be uncertain whether the annual benefits are plus or minus 30 percent of the mean. No correlation means that overestimates are likely to be compensated by underestimates. Perfect positive correlation of all successive benefits means, however, that

---

[10] In all the equations presented here it is assumed that $V(e_t)$ is the same in all years, i.e. $V(e_1) = V(e_2) = \ldots = V(e_n)$, where e_t is the random effect.

the same forces are at work, and if we have overestimated the benefits in the first year overestimation will occur in all subsequent years.

To compare variances it is frequently convenient to use the ratio $C = \sqrt{V(B)}/\bar{B}$, the so-called coefficient of variation. C is then a measure of the relative variance and allows us to make some general statements about the impact of various kinds of uncertainty on the uncertainty implied for the overall returns for a project.

The coefficient of variation of the present value, C_R, when successive benefits are perfectly correlated simply equals the coefficient of variation of the annual benefits, C_B, i.e.

$$\frac{\sqrt{V(R)}}{\bar{R}} = \frac{\sum a^t \sqrt{V(B)}}{\sum a^t \bar{B}} \qquad (24)$$

or

$$C_R = C_B$$

However, if successive benefits are not correlated, the coefficient of variation of the present value is

$$C_R = (\sqrt{\sum a^{2t}}/\sum a^t)\, C_B \qquad (25)$$

Table 4 gives the ratio of the coefficients of variation of the present value to the coefficient of variation of the annual benefits for selected life spans of projects and discount rates. As is to be expected, the longer the life of the project and the lower the discount rate, the more "errors" of estimation in the true benefits compensate for each other. Quite generally, Table 4 shows that year to year variations in benefits, perhaps due to weather or other non-systematic errors (in terms of persistence over time), are relatively quite unimportant in assessing the uncertainty about the present value (or rate of return). In general, the standard deviation of the present value derived from a given standard deviation of year to year correlated annual benefits will be approximately 3 to 4 times as large as when derived from the same standard deviation of year to year uncorrelated benefits.

TABLE 4: Ratio of Coefficient of Variation of Present Value (C_R) to Coefficient of Variation of Successively Uncorrelated Annual Benefits (C_B)
(for a stream of equal mean annual benefits)

Number of Years	Discount Rate		
	6%	10%	20%
	C_R/C_B equals:		
10	.32	.33	.34
20	.24	.25	.31
30	.20	.23	

A coefficient of variation as large as 0.5, for instance, in the annual benefits deriving from year to year uncorrelated "errors" about an assumed estimated mean level of benefits, would result in a coefficient of variation of approximately only 0.15 in present value. In other words a 95 percent confidence statement (approximately plus and minus 2 standard deviations, assuming a normal distribution), such that the annual benefits might be fluctuating within a range of 0 to 200, would reduce to a similarly defined confidence statement that the present value of the stream of benefits will be within the range of 700 to 1,300. Whereas, if successive annual benefits were perfectly correlated, the corresponding confidence statement with respect to the present value of the stream of benefits would have given a range of 0 to 2,000.

For another illustration of the effect of correlation consider the data in Table 5. The benefits in this case are accruing over an eight-year period. The discount rate is assumed to be 8 percent. If successive values of the benefits are not correlated the variance of the present value is 1,187 and the standard deviation 34. Uncorrelated benefits would be an appropriate assumption, if the source of the variability of outcome is a result of year to year changes in climate or prices which in turn are not correlated. If, however, the uncertainty is for instance the direct consequence of not knowing consumer reaction to a new product, the benefit can be assumed to be almost perfectly correlated. That is, in each of the 8 years benefits may be high or low, but if consumers respond unfavorably the benefits will be low in every year, and if the new product is favorably received the benefits will be high in every year. Assuming perfect correlation, the same assumptions about the variances of the benefits in each year will result in a variance of the present value of 9,149 or a standard deviation of 96.

That uncorrelated fluctuations in annual benefits are relatively unim-

TABLE 5: Hypothetical Data for Calculating a Variance of the Present Value when Benefits from Successive Years are Uncorrelated or Perfectly Correlated

t	a^t	a^{2t}	$V(B_t)$	$\sqrt{V(B_t)}$	$V(R)$
1	.93	.86	225	15	*Uncorrelated*
2	.86	.74	400	20	$V(R) = 1,187$
3	.79	.63	225	15	Standard Deviation
4	.74	.54	200	14	$(\sqrt{V(R)}) = 34$
5	.68	.46	256	16	*Correlated*
6	.63	.40	289	17	$V(R) = 9,149$
7	.58	.34	324	18	Standard Deviation
8	.54	.29	361	19	$(\sqrt{V(R)}) = 96$

Elasticity of Variance of Present Value of a Stream of Benefits with Respect to Variance of Successively Uncorrelated Benefits (when $B_t = B + e_t$)

Duration of Benefits (years)	Discount Rate		
	6%	10%	20%
	(1) $V(e_t) = V(B)$		
10	.093	.097	.098
20	.053	.060	.088
30	.040	.051	—
	(2) $V(e_t) = 2\,V(B)$		
10	.171	.177	.180
20	.100	.114	.163
30	.076	.097	—
	(3) $V(e_t) = 3\,V(B)$		
10	.236	.244	.245
20	.143	.162	.225
30	.111	.138	—

portant for the uncertainty about the present value (or rate of return on the project) can be shown by considering the simultaneous contribution of the variances from successively correlated and uncorrelated benefits on the variance of the present value of a stream of benefits. If the variance is an additive function of the variance in the level of benefits and the variance due to year to year fluctuations such that

$$V(B_t) = V(B) + V(e_t) \qquad (26)$$

Correspondingly, the variance of the present value of such a stream of benefits is

$$V(R) = \left(\sum a^t\right)^2 V(B) + \left(\sum a^{2t}\right) V(e_t) \qquad (27)$$

To measure the relative sensitivity of the variance of present value to variances from different sources it is now useful to calculate elasticities, i.e. the percentage change in the variance of the present value to a one percent change in the variance of a contributing factor.[11] When the factors are

---

[11] The elasticity (E) of $V(R)$ with respect to $V(e_t)$ is as follows:

$$E_{V(e_t)} = \cfrac{1}{1 + \cfrac{\left(\sum a^t\right)^2}{\sum a^{2t}} \cdot \cfrac{V(B)}{V(e_t)}}$$

These elasticities for various interest rates and relative sizes of $V(e_t)$ are presented in Table 6. The elasticity of $V(R)$ with respect to $V(B)$ is: $1 - E_{V(e_t)}$.

additive and not correlated, these elasticities add up to unity. Table 6 gives elasticities of the coefficient of variation of the present value with respect to the coefficient of variation of the successively uncorrelated benefits. Clearly, unless the project life is very short and the year to year fluctuations are very large relative to the uncertainty about the level of benefits, the variance of the present value is quite insensitive to the projected year to year uncorrelated variations in benefits.

For an illustration, consider an irrigation project whose life is 20 years while the discount rate is 10 percent. The average expected annual return is not known with any certainty, but is estimated to be a normal distribution with a mean of 100 and a standard deviation of 10. Furthermore, no matter what average level of returns will actually occur, there are expected year to year fluctuations. If the standard deviation of these fluctuations is also 10, the total variance of the present value turns out to be about 30,800 (the mean of the distribution of present value is 850 and the standard deviation is 175). Neglecting the year to year uncorrelated errors the variance would have been 28,960 and the standard deviation 170. Hence, the uncorrelated year to year variations "contribute" only 6 percent to the variance of the present value. The elasticity with respect to these fluctuations in Table 6 is .06.

Annual benefits contain an uncertain trend

One case of strong serial correlation in connection with variances of annual benefits is, of course, the presence of trend, i.e. the uncertainty about benefits derived in a particular year arises primarily from not knowing the trend. Benefits may increase over time because a structure must be constructed to an excessive capacity which will be only increasingly used with time, or in general, because of an increase in demand over time for the services generated by the investment. Benefits may also decline because of progressive physical or technological obsolescence of the investment. For illustration, let us imagine that an annual benefit (B_t) can be represented by the following equation:

$$B_t = B_0 + bt + e_t \qquad (28)$$

where B_0 is the benefit in the initial year, b is the annual growth and, t is the number of years since the initial benefits have occurred and e_t represents many random effects which can make an annual benefit deviate from its normal trend.

Given the growth-of-benefits equation (28) the formula for calculating the mean and variance of present value ($\bar{R}$ and $V(R)$), based on knowledge of $\bar{B}_0$ and $V(B_0)$, $\bar{b}$ and $V(b)$ and $V(e)$ ($\bar{e}$ is assumed to be zero) are as follows:

$$\bar{R} = \left(\sum a^t\right) \bar{B}_0 + \left(\sum ta^t\right) \bar{b} \tag{29}$$

and

$$V(R) = \left(\sum a^t\right)^2 V(B_0) + \left(\sum ta^t\right)^2 V(b) + \left(\sum a^{2t}\right) V(e_t) \tag{30}$$

On the basis of the above equations, it is first interesting to note the relative sensitivity of $\bar{R}$ to $\bar{B}_0$, the initial level of benefits and to $\bar{b}$, the annual average growth. Here again we use the elasticity concept, i.e. the percentage change in the mean present value in response to the percentage change in the mean growth, etc. Obviously, this sensitivity depends on the relative size of the annual growth, the discount rate and the life of the project. Table 7 gives the elasticity with respect to changes in $\bar{b}$, the growth rate for two levels. The high level corresponds with a doubling of the initial

TABLE 7: Elasticity of the Mean Present Value ($\bar{R}$) with Respect to Mean Growth ($\bar{b}$) and Mean Initial Benefits ($\bar{B}$)[a]

Project Life	Elasticity with Respect to:	Discount Rate		
		6%	10%	20%
	High Average Annual Growth $\left(\bar{b} = \dfrac{B_0}{10}\right)$			
10 years	$\bar{b}$	.33	.32	.29
	$\bar{B}_0$	.67	.68	.71
20 years	$\bar{b}$	.46	.43	.35
	$\bar{B}_0$	.54	.57	.65
30 years	$\bar{b}$	.53	.48	.37
	$\bar{B}_0$	.47	.52	.63
	Low Average Annual Growth $\left(\bar{b} = \dfrac{B_0}{20}\right)$			
10 years	$\bar{b}$	.20	.19	.17
	$\bar{B}_0$	.80	.81	.83
20 years	$\bar{b}$	.30	.27	.21
	$\bar{B}_0$	.70	.73	.79
30 years	$\bar{b}$	.36	.32	.23
	$\bar{B}_0$	.64	.68	.77

[a] The elasticity of $\bar{R}$ with respect to $\bar{b} = \dfrac{1}{1 + \dfrac{\left(\sum a^t\right)}{\left(\sum ta^t\right)} \cdot \dfrac{B_0}{\bar{b}}}$

benefits in ten years (i.e. $\bar{b} = \bar{B}_0/10$) and the low rate implies a doubling of the initial benefits by the twentieth year (i.e. $\bar{b} = \bar{B}_0/20$). For instance, given a project life of 10 years, a low growth rate and a 20 percent discount rate, a 10 percent change in the annual growth would change the present value only 1.7 percent, whereas with a project life of thirty years, a high growth rate and a 6 percent discount rate the present value would change by 5.3 percent. Conversely, in the first case a 10 percent change in the initial level of benefits, $\bar{B}_0$, would change the present value by 8.3 percent, and in the second case by only 4.7 percent. (The two elasticities always add up to unity.)

Table 8 illustrates the order of magnitude of the relative sensitivity of the variance of present value with respect to variances in b, B_0 and e.[12] Throughout the assumption is that the relative variances of B_0, B and e are the same; in particular, it has been assumed that the coefficient of variations of B_0 and b are 0.25. Thus if $\bar{B}_0$ is 10 and $\bar{b}$ is 1, the respective standard deviation is 2.5 and .25, and the standard deviation of e_t is assumed to be 2.5 as well. The high annual growth assumes a doubling of benefits every ten years, the low growth rate a doubling of benefits every twenty years. The elasticities given in Table 8 illustrate that the variance is most sensitive to the variance of B_0.

This is, of course, to be expected since an error in the level of benefits would have a constant effect on the present value each year, whereas an error in the annual growth would have little effect in the early years and a large effect in subsequent years when, due to discounting for time, it matters much less. Particularly noteworthy is the relative lack of sensitivity of present value estimates to year-to-year uncorrelated errors. This means, for instance, that for the purpose of predicting the present value for a fertilizer project, one can predict quite precisely if one knows the yield response to fertilizer under average weather conditions and it matters little that in some years the benefits will be much higher than in others due to uncorrelated fluctuations in climatic conditions.

---

[12] The elasticities of the present value with respect to the variances of B_0, b and e, $E_{V(B_0)}$, $E_{V(b)}$, and $E_{V(e_t)}$ are as follows:

$$E_{V(B_0)} = \cfrac{1}{1 + \cfrac{(\sum ta^t)^2}{(\sum a^t)^2} \cdot \cfrac{V(b)}{V(B_0)} + \cfrac{(\sum a^{2t})}{(\sum a^t)^2} \cdot \cfrac{V(e_t)}{V(B_0)}}$$

$$E_{V(b)} = \cfrac{1}{1 + \cfrac{(\sum a^t)^2}{(\sum ta^t)^2} \cdot \cfrac{V(B_0)}{V(B)} + \cfrac{(\sum a^{2t})}{(\sum ta^t)^2} \cdot \cfrac{V(e_t)}{V(b)}}$$

and

$$E_{V(e_t)} = \cfrac{1}{1 + \cfrac{(\sum a^t)^2}{(\sum a^{2t})} \cdot \cfrac{V(B)}{V(e_t)} + \cfrac{(\sum ta^t)^2}{(\sum a^{2t})} \cdot \cfrac{V(b)}{V(e_t)}}$$

TABLE 8: Elasticities of the Variance of Present Value $V(R)$ with Respect to $V(b)$, $V(\bar{B}_0)$ and $V(e)$.

Project Life	Elasticity of $V(R)$ with Respect to:	Discount Rate 6%	10%	20%
	High Average Annual Growth $\left(\bar{b} = \dfrac{\bar{B}_0}{10} \right)$			
10 years	$V(b)$	.19	.17	.13
	$V(B_0)$	.74	.75	.78
	$V(e_t)$	.07	.08	.09
20 years	$V(b)$	.41	.34	.21
	$V(B_0)$	.57	.61	.76
	$V(e_t)$	.02	.05	.03
	Low Average Annual Growth $\left(\bar{b} = \dfrac{\bar{B}_0}{20} \right)$			
10 years	$V(b)$	.05	.05	.04
	$V(B_0)$	.86	.86	.87
	$V(e_t)$	.09	.09	.09
20 years	$V(b)$	.15	.12	.06
	$V(B_0)$	.81	.83	.85
	$V(e_t)$	.04	.05	.09

Life of project

One source of uncertainty may be the life of a project. Let us say that because of silting of a reservoir it is not known whether its usefulness will be terminated after ten, twenty or thirty years. Quite generally, of course, concern about uncertainty from this source becomes less important when the discount rate is high and the earliest date of termination is quite a long time in the future. If the discount rate is 10 percent, for instance, the present value of benefits is hardly affected by whether the life of the project is thirty or fifty years.

If the uncertainty about project life is high, the project life is relatively short and the discount rate fairly high, the usual practice of using the median life of the project in calculating benefits can, in fact, be quite misleading in terms of what is realistically expected to happen. To illustrate the problem, consider a project which results in equal annual benefits of 1,000 dollars. The life of the project is assumed to be anywhere from 10 to 30 years, any number of years within this range believed to be equally likely. If one then calculates the gross benefits, assuming a twenty year life of project, the present value of the benefits is 8,514 dollars. Although the chances of a longer life and consequently higher benefits, and a shorter life and lower benefits are 50–50, the expected gains would not be offset by the expected losses. In fact, the "true" expected present value, i.e. $\bar{R}$, is 8,253 dollars. Furthermore, the chance of realizing a present value which is 1,000 dollars less than the one projected based on the median life of the project is about 30 percent, whereas the chance of getting 1,000 dollars more is zero.

Estimating probability distributions of annual benefits

Attention in this section focuses on selected general problems in estimating the probability distribution of the benefits in each year by aggregating probability distributions of various factors. Besides being the building blocks for estimating present value of the project, the probability distributions of the annual benefits may be of interest as such. A high return in one year may not compensate fully for a low return in another year for many reasons although the average return is satisfactory. It is often assumed that unstable benefits from year to year are less desirable than a stream of benefits of equal annual magnitudes, because the cost of borrowing is higher than the rate of return on savings or because of diminishing marginal utility of income. It is just possible, however, that a nation may prefer a project which yields unstable returns over the years. Consider for instance a nation which must decide between two projects which over the years would produce an equal amount of food per dollar invested. It would be quite in the national interest to prefer a project with a highly fluctuating food output, if this nation could count on getting food grants (or soft loans) in years when its domestic food supply was insufficient to feed the population, and if in food surplus years the surpluses could be effectively used for generating investment and economic growth.

Estimation of the annual benefits involves a careful accounting of many variables and relationships between variables. It is not possible to give any general rules for deciding how many variables and relationships should be explicitly considered. A probability appraisal may sometimes suggest consideration of more variables and relationships than would be otherwise explicitly considered, as it is sometimes easier to assess the probability distribution of a simple than that of a more complex event. However, generally it is sufficient to estimate the probability distributions of the variables and parameters which one would consider implicitly without probability appraisal.

The major problem in estimating the aggregated probability distribution of the annual benefits is once again correlation. Say the annual operating costs are estimated by summing costs of various inputs. The uncertainty about each cost item arises from not knowing exactly (a) what quantity of the input will be needed and (b) the price of the input. Both the quantities and the prices will often be partially correlated. Only a careful examination of the data and a thorough understanding of the underlying relationships can lead to realistic appraisal of the approximate extent of correlation.

It is not possible to give rules for estimating correlations, just as it is impossible to give general rules for estimating probability distributions. The point to be made here is simply to suggest that the estimated and reported cost-benefit measure of a project should adequately reflect what the project appraisers believe to be their best judgment about the correlation between probability distributions as well as the nature of the probability distributions themselves. Otherwise a careful probability analysis may be self-defeating, or in fact misleading. That is to say, if a probability distribution of a complicated event is to be estimated by aggregating probability distributions, all correlations must be explicitly considered. Otherwise the gains from explicit consideration of many probability distributions may be offset by the loss from neglecting correlations which would be implicitly taken into account by a less disaggregated analysis.

Often a large number of costs and benefits are summed to derive the total net benefit. If one assumes no correlation when in fact the different costs and revenues are perfectly correlated, the true variance may be as much as n times the estimated variance when n benefits are summed up, i.e. when two benefits are aggregated the true variance may be two times the estimated variance, and when ten revenues and costs are aggregated the true variance may be ten times the estimated variance. When many correlations are negative, the true variance may be zero or much less than the estimated variance.[13]

Summary and Conclusions on Aggregation of Probability Distributions

(a) Judgments about the likelihoods of various outcomes of the elementary events affecting the costs and benefits from a project can

---

[13] Assuming $B = B_1 + B_2 + \ldots + B_n$

and $\qquad B_2 = a_2 B_1, \ldots, B_n = a_n B_1$

then the true variance of B is

$$V(B) = (1 + a_2 + \ldots + a_n)^2 \, V(B_1)$$

whereas, if it were assumed that $[B_1, B_2], \ldots [B_1, B_n]$ are not correlated, the variance of B would have been calculated as

$$V(B) = (1 + a_2^2 + \ldots + a_n^2) \, (VB_1)$$

Note that $V(B)/V(B)$ is at maximum when $a_i = 1$, i.e. when the marginal cost of capital (or time discount used) is taken to be nil.

be combined without great difficulty into an estimate of the approximate probability distribution of the net present value or the internal rate of return.

(b) There are available basically two approaches for aggregating probability distributions into an estimate of the probability distribution of returns from a project: the simulation by a high-speed computer of a sample of outcomes based on randomly selected sets of observations from the probability distributions of inputs, and the mathematical approach of aggregating mathematical expectations into an estimate of the mean and variance of a project's returns.

(c) For most operational purposes the simulation procedure is the only feasible method at this time. The simulation procedure requires no prior assumptions about the nature of the aggregated probability distribution and no mathematical skills on the part of project appraisers. The major disadvantage of the procedure is the fact that resulting estimates are specific to one set of input distributions.

(d) A major advantage of the mathematical approach elaborated in this chapter is that the mean and variance (or standard deviation) calculations can be made quickly for relatively simple projects when only a crude estimate of a project's returns based on a few crucial variables is needed or feasible. The method is useful for deriving generalizations about the sensitivity of estimates to various elementary events.

(e) Year to year uncorrelated fluctuations are of relatively minor importance in terms of the probability distribution of overall project benefits. Instead, one should concentrate on making sure that uncertainty about the persistent level of costs and benefits is properly taken into account.

(f) Generally, the problem of estimating the extent of correlation between the various probability distributions of the elementary events is likely to prove the most difficult aspect in application of the procedure. When one estimates directly the probability distribution of a complicated event (like the rate of return of an investment) correlations are implicitly taken into account. If such a distribution is estimated, however, from synthesizing the effects of various contributing factors, correlations must be made explicit and taken into account. Otherwise, the gains from disaggregation must be seriously questioned.

42

(g) Probability appraisal is important, not only for estimating the en-
     tire probability distribution of the return from an investment, but
     should be employed also when interest focuses on only the most
     likely return. The usual practice of aggregating averages or most
     probable values of a series of events may in fact *not* yield a correct
     estimate of the average or most likely returns of a project as
     intended.

(h) Just as any quantification of economic relationship is generally only
     a question of more or less rather than yes or no, so the optimum
     extent of quantification of the uncertain elements in project ap-
     praisal will differ from case to case. In a project appraisal, the
     importance of quantifying uncertainty depends not only on the
     usual limitations of time, effect and cost, but also on the specific
     decision context. If the project is one of many unrelated projects
     it may be less important to quantify uncertainty than when the
     project is very large relative to a country's investment program.

IV

PROJECT DECISIONS
UNDER UNCERTAINTY

Introduction

After having shown how to incorporate uncertainty into the appraisal of projects and portions of projects, we should consider how and to what extent such appraisals might be useful for the evaluation of public projects, i.e. for decisions. As indicated earlier, outcomes of decisions which are affected by the interaction of a great many noncontrollable variables are most adequately described in terms of probability distribution and sometimes quite adequately by means and variances.[1] For this reason, and because the objective of this paper is to focus primarily on the appraisal of large-scale publicly financed projects, only decision theories which relate to choices between probability distributions of outcomes (specifically, means and variances) are discussed here.

Quite apart from the decision problems encountered in the general evaluation of projects, there are certain decisions which can only be intelligently evaluated if one explicitly studies probability distributions. These are

---

[1] The characterization of probability distributions in terms of means and variances will be seen to be sufficient for some types of distributions, specifically when a normal distribution is approximated, and regardless of normality, if the decision-maker wishes to maximize expected utility and the utility function of income is quadratic.

44

problems of sequential decisions and certain timing aspects of investments and the whole subject of the value of gathering additional information. These subjects will also be briefly discussed below.

The first reason for making such appraisals, as indicated in the previous chapter, is of course, quite intuitively, that decision-makers want to know the most likely or average outcome as well as the extent of the riskiness of a project, and a probability distribution or the mean and variance are convenient indices. The fact that decision-makers ask for this kind of information is sufficient evidence that decisions are affected by it. If this information is not supplied by those who are in a position to know best, second-rate information may be substituted. On the other hand, if instead of supplying means and variances, the appraiser himself adjusts the estimate of the outcome of a project by some uncertainty factor, the organization is not unlikely to reach investment decisions which are inconsistent and misguided in terms of higher level policy objectives.

Any theory of economic choice involves the following basic ingredients: (1) the decision agent's preference function, (2) his basic endowment and (3) alternative courses of action with specified consequences. The interaction between these three aspects of a decision problem can be best illustrated by a simple hypothetical example.

A Hypothetical Example of the Decision Problem

Consider an individual who is told that he has been selected to receive a prize, and that it is his prerogative to choose between several options. Assume furthermore, that the same individual has zero wealth and that it is two days before he will receive his next monthly salary. By option (A) he will receive 10 dollars at once. Options (B) and (C) will each consist of two possible outcomes, to be decided by the tossing of a fair coin. By option (B) he would have a 50–50 chance of getting 5 or 15 dollars, respectively. Option (C) would yield him 0 or 20 dollars, each with a 50–50 chance. The need for survival would pretty much rule out the latter option. The recipient's choice between options (A) and (B) would depend on his subjective preference. If he likes to gamble, or expressed in another way, if his marginal utility is an increasing function of income, he will choose option (B).

Consider now a second, somewhat different situation in which the same individual is told that his options are to receive (A) a prize of 1,000 dollars at once, (B) 990 dollars at once plus a 50–50 chance of 5 or 15 dollars and (C) 990 dollars at once plus a 50–50 chance of 0 or 20 dollars, respectively. Clearly, one distinguishing characteristic between the first and the second situation is the fact that by comparison the decision problem appears to be a trivial one in the latter case. Yet, note that in both instances, the course of action and their consequences are identical: 10 dollars for certain vs. 5 and 15, or 0 to 20 with a 50–50 chance respectively. The difference comes, of course, in the endowment, i.e. the variability of outcomes relative to the total outcomes is small even for the option involving the largest gamble. Hence, it is quite conceivable that the same individual who prefers (A) or (B) to (C) in the first case, will this time prefer option (C) to either (A) or (B).

In a third case, we might conceive of the same individual confronted with having to choose between (A) receipt of 1,000 dollars at once, (B) a 50–50 chance of receiving 500 dollars or 1,500 dollars, and (C) a 50–50 chance at receiving nothing or 2,000 dollars. The endowment and the variability relative to the average of the respective outcomes in this situation are approximately the same as in the first cited case. However, it is not at all unlikely that the decision would not be the same as in the first case. In fact, we probably would not be too surprised if the same individual who would have chosen option (B) in the first case would prefer (A) in this case. This means that an individual's preference function is not a given datum at all but may vary with the magnitudes of the options.

Finally, we may conceive of a fourth situation in which the same individual is given the option of receiving 1,000 dollars at once, or alternatively of participating in a game of chance in which his payoff is to be determined by tossing a coin one hundred times. Under option (B) he would receive in each toss either 6 or 16 dollars. Option (C) would pay him 0 to 24 dollars. Clearly, these uncertainty options are different from the ones described in the first three cases. The total payoffs are likely to approximate one hundred times the average payoff, i.e. 1,100 and 1,200 dollars for options (B) and (C), respectively. Since the total payoff for option (B) can be expected to approximate a normal probability distribution with a standard deviation of about 50, we would have in fact a 98 percent confidence that the payoff from (B) would be greater than 1,000 dollars. Except for an extremely conservative individual, it is therefore quite clear that (B) would be preferred to (A) and most likely (C) would be considered still more desirable than (B).[2] As a generalization of this case, it may be stated

---

[2] Note that: $E(B_i) = (.5) (6) + (.5) (16) = 11$
$\text{Var } (B_i) = .5 (6 - 11)^2 + .5 (16 - 11)^2 = 25$
and $E(B) = 100 \, E(B_i) = (100) (11) = 1,100$
$\text{Var } (B) = 100 \, \text{Var } (B_i) = (110) (25) = 2,500$
Standard deviation $(B) = 50$
Similarly, $E(C_i) = (.5) (0) + (.5) (24) = 12$

that if plans of action are compared whose outcomes are the sum total of many small uncertain outcomes, the decision may be based on a comparison of the expected outcome from each plan, and the same optimization rules which apply to ordering courses of action with certain outcomes are relevant for this particular kind of uncertainty problem.

Project Appraisal and Utility Theory

To gain some perspective on the nature of economic decision problems under uncertainty it is worthwhile to distinguish first of all between the decision problem of an individual and of society in a deterministic world, and then to superimpose the problem of uncertain consequences from alternative courses of action.

Very generally, the objective of economic activity may be regarded as one of maximizing utility or welfare. Utility need not be a measurable object in order to derive meaningful criteria for an individual's economic decisions. Instead, it suffices to assume that utility is an increasing function of income to see that profit maximization is consistent with utility maximization. In a world of certainty, planning for an individual would in fact involve no decision problem at all. The investment appraiser would examine the income (or returns) from alternative courses of action and, presumably, the one with the highest returns would be chosen.

Planning for society is more ambiguous, even in a deterministic world. At best, it can be said that given the same minimal assumptions about utility (being an increasing function of income for each member of society), society would be *potentially* better off by maximizing income (Pareto Optimum). That is, if we abstract from possible interdependence of utility and if the gainers from a particular course of action were actually to compensate the losers, social utility would be maximized by maximizing overall income.[3] In reality, compensation does not usually take place. Hence, public investment decisions usually require a balancing of preferences for a certain income distribution and maximizing overall income.

In dealing with economic choices involving uncertain outcomes, it is

---

$$\text{Var } (C_i) = .5 \ (0 - 12)^2 + .5 \ (24 - 12)^2 = 144$$
and
$$E(C) = (100) \ (12) = 1,200$$
$$\text{Var } (C) = 100 \ (144) = 14,400$$
$$\text{Standard deviation } (C) = 120.$$

[3] Conversely, if utility could be actually measured (not only ordinally in terms of relative preferences) it would be possible to derive a social utility function. However, most economists would agree that the notion of measuring absolute utility of individuals, quite apart from the impossible task of aggregating, is quite obsolete.

necessary to know something more about an individual's utility function. Presumably, it is possible to determine an individual's utility function with respect to uncertain incomes. To be sure, such a utility function measures relative utility and not absolute utility, that is, the scale on which utility is measured has no known origin.[4] By this theory, the objective of the individual is to maximize expected utility. If an individual's utility function is linear, expected utility is maximized whenever he chooses the course of action which maximizes his expected income. Otherwise, when the utility function is curvilinear, it is necessary to know the probability distributions of income from alternative courses of action in order to ascertain which course maximizes expected utility. If the utility function can be approximated (in the relevant range) by a quadratic function, expected utility is a function of the mean and variance of income, i.e. if

$$U = a_0 + a_1 I + a_2 I^2 \tag{1}$$

then

$$E(U) = a_0 + a_1 E(I) + a_2 \left(V(I) + (E(I))^2 \right) \tag{2}$$

where U is utility and I is income, and $E(I)$ and $V(I)$ are the mean and the variance of the probability distribution of income, respectively.

The risk averter or "conservative" individual would have a utility function which increases at a decreasing rate, such that $a_2 < 0$ and, hence, the expected utility is a decreasing function of the variance (the larger the uncertainty, the lower the expected utility). On the other hand, the risk taker's or gambler's utility function increases at an increasing rate, and hence his expected utility is an increasing function of the variance of income.

One immediate consequence of the expected utility theory is, of course, that decision-makers do need to or ought to know means and variances (if not complete probability distributions) of returns from alternative investments. Beyond this, however, whether the utility function of an individual can ever be adequately measured and whether the individual can be observed to behave consistently with that function so as to make this a predictive or explanatory theory is a question which is beyond the scope of this paper. Furthermore, we also do not concern ourselves here with the

---

[4] This is the most widely accepted theory about man's behaviour in economic risk situations since von Neumann and Morgenstern published their *Theory of Games and Economic Behavior*. For a very lucid and non-mathematical exposition of the nature of the theory and how to measure cardinal utility functions the reader is referred to Ralph O. Swalm's paper, "Utility Theory—Insights into Risk Taking," *Harvard Business Review*, November–December 1966.

question of which utility functions are or are not compatible with the static and dynamic theory of a free enterprise system.

Before we attempt to summarize the implications of the appraisal and evaluation of projects subject to uncertainties in the context of public decisions, it is interesting to note how the expected utility approach has been evaluated in the context of large US corporations. In a recent study, R. O. Swalm[5] estimated segments of utility functions by quizzing one hundred executives, of which a large number belonged to one corporation. The participating executives were asked to make choices (between courses of action which would lead to outcomes with different degrees of riskiness) in their capacities as corporate decision-makers, not as private individuals dealing with their own funds. Furthermore, they were asked to tell what they would *actually do* and not what they feel they *ought to do*. Briefly, the most significant findings were:

(a) The measured utility functions reveal widely different attitudes towards risk taking (even for the executives making decisions for one and the same corporation).

(b) The sample revealed differences in utility functions ranging from one which would characterize an extremely conservative individual to one which would be characteristic of a gambler.

(c) Most respondents tended to be extremely conservative when chances for negative returns were involved.

(d) The executives' utility functions seem to have been more closely related to the amounts with which the respondents were accustomed to deal as individuals than to the financial position of the company.

From these major findings the author concludes that:

Businessmen do *not* attempt to optimize the expected dollar outcome in risk situations involving what, to them, are large amounts.

Cardinal utility theory offers a reasonable basis for judging the internal consistency of a series of decisions.

The theory offers a relatively simple way of classifying many types of industrial decision-makers. For example, a supervisor may learn that, in decisions involving significant risks, one man tends to be quite conservative, a second tends to be a gambler, and a third tends to be moderately

---

[5] R. O. Swalm, *ibid.*

conservative. If he is moderately conservative himself, he will be happier delegating decisions to the third than to either of the other two.

The action a junior executive recommends in a risk situation is a function of his own 'planning horizon' . . . rather than of the financial condition and position of his company.

If the decision-makers interviewed are at all representative of U.S. executives in general, our managers are surely not the takers of risk so often alluded to in the classical defense of the capitalistic system. Rather than seeking risks, they shun them, consistently refusing to recommend risks, that, from the overall company viewpoint, would almost surely be attractive.

What, if any, are the implications of all this for project appraisal and evaluation of public decisions in general? Basically, the problems are similar. The only difference, an important one to be sure, is the additional difficulty of defining and measuring the utility function of society. Even if somehow we knew how to make interpersonal utility comparisons, that is, even if we knew the weights to be used in aggregating utilities, there remains the problem that cardinal utility as proposed by von Neumann and Morgenstern is a relative rather than absolute measure of utility and, hence, cannot be additive. There is, therefore, no way of deriving the shape of society's utility function from the utility functions of individuals. One way of ascertaining a utility function which might reflect at least the wishes of the controlling segment of the population (be it the majority or a minority) may be through trial and error and the political process. That is, the decision-makers in government may learn from experience whether the public's disapproval of projects which have disappointed is more or less intensely offset by the public's applause for projects which have succeeded beyond expectations.

The slow disappearance of risk takers and its consequences for the growth potential of the capitalistic system may be a matter of concern with respect to governmental as well as corporate decisions to the extent that decisions are made by lower echelons who might not be sufficiently rewarded for unusually successful projects but are reprimanded for failures. In this context, it is worthwhile to remember, however, that whether an activity involving risk is undertaken or shelved depends not only on the attitude of the decision-maker but equally on whether or not the risks of many independent activities can be pooled. The best example is, of course, in the field of research and development activities. If an individual's payoff were to depend on whether he succeeds in inventing a process to copy nature's photosynthesis, even a gambling spirit might be discouraged from undertaking an activity with such a high chance of failure. By contrast, a research laboratory manager with a much more conservative attitude towards risk might not hesitate to employ the same individual together with 1,000 other research workers assigned to other projects, because the chance of the whole operation failing becomes so much smaller than that of a single project failing.

The important thing here is that the riskiness of the project should be evaluated at the top level (together with other projects), and that, to the extent that the decision process must be diffused, the lower echelon decision makers should not be unduly reprimanded for failures and should not fail to be applauded and rewarded for successful outcomes. In any case, to appraise attitudes as well as the performance of an organization, it would seem to be of vital importance to know the riskiness of various projects and also the specific sources of the risks in order to make at least an informed judgment about the likely joint outcomes from a total investment program.

Public Investment Decisions

Fortunately for those having to advise on the selection of government financed projects (and the author of this paper) the kind of uncertainty decisions frequently encountered by governments are those described by the second and fourth case in the hypothetical example presented earlier. A government's investment plan consists frequently of many diverse projects with uncorrelated risks, and as long as the objective is to maximize the sum of the benefits, neither the risk preference function nor the exact probability distributions of the outcomes from each project need to be known. As long as the utility is an increasing function of benefits, the government will want to choose the projects with the highest expected benefits. In these cases, compensating risks can be relied upon to assure that the expected benefits will be approximately realized.

A government's investment plan may also be frequently viewed as analogous with the case of a small gamble offered to a well endowed individual. In this case, it matters not how large the variances of alternative projects are relative to their expected values, but rather it is the variance of alternative projects relative to the total revenue of the nation which matters. Since benefits from projects are likely to result in only a small net addition to the total revenue, even fairly large differences in the variances from various projects are not likely to be important considerations when viewed relatively to the total revenues, even if the risks are not compensated elsewhere in the economy.

Unfortunately, on more careful examination, the uncertainty issue involved in project appraisal is far from adequately represented by the two types of gambling situations described in the previous paragraphs. Let us then take up one by one the kind of project decisions which must be appraised in terms of probability distributions of outcomes and preference functions of the decision agents, or else require consideration of the probability distributions of selected variables affecting the expected outcome of a project.

Large Specialized Projects or Aggregates of Smaller Projects whose Outcomes are Highly Correlated. A plan which consists of a few large projects is not necessarily more uncertain in its consequences than a plan consisting of many small projects, except if the consequences of the large projects are fairly uncertain and the outcomes of the small projects are uncorrelated. The size of the project by itself is no indication of the anticipated variability of outcomes. It is rather the degree of specialization which is likely to increase its riskiness. A large infrastructure project, for instance, whose benefits depend on many independent variables is more likely to realize the expected outcome (if properly estimated) than a highly specialized industry, whose benefits might depend almost entirely on an uncertain export market for a particular commodity. An infrastructure project may, of course, be affected by many variables which are highly correlated, say the demand for different commodities which all depend in turn primarily on GNP, and its projected benefits would then be nearly as uncertain as the forecast of GNP. Viewed then in terms of the total benefits from an aggregation of public projects and assuming that at least when it comes to the evaluation of outcomes for an entire investment plan the preference is to avert risk, caution must be exercised to select not so much projects which have a small variance by themselves, but rather those whose outcomes are not highly correlated. In other words, one should seek not so much to avoid risky projects as to seek out compensating risks. A risk averting preference, of course, merely means that the decision-maker is willing to give up some expected income for a smaller variance of income, where the terms of this trade depend on the decision-maker's subjective preference. What interests us for project appraisal is the fact that the evaluation of a project within an overall plan in terms of riskiness requires knowledge not only of the variance of that project but more importantly of the sources of the variance, which permits those who are charged with evaluating the variance of the total investment plan to calculate the covariance among various project alternatives.

The Impact of Failures and Successes of a Project not Compensated by Failures and Successes of Other Projects. Perhaps the most important reason for having to worry about uncertain outcomes from a project is the fact that the expected utility derived from a government's total investment plan is not merely a function of total income, but rather is an aggregation of the expected utilities derived from each project.[6] Hence, the compensation for other than expected outcomes from a project, whether through compensating errors or the fact that a project merely supplements a large income (or wealth) from other sources, should not be taken for granted. Some reasons why compensation may be incomplete, i.e. income may not be additive are:

(a) The value of additional income may not be the same for different individuals or regions and projects typically affect different individuals and regions.

(b) Failure of individual projects may have psychological and political impacts which are not compensated by unusual successes of other projects, and vice versa.

(c) Projects may have to meet specific supply targets which due to various capital or foreign exchange restrictions cannot be reflected additively when distributions of returns from various investments are aggregated. For the same reason variability of returns from year to year may be a consideration in evaluating the expected utility of a particular project.[7]

There are then at least some uncertainty environment and decision problems for which it is sufficient to know the expected (average) outcome of each of the alternative courses of action to choose between them. In such cases, the preference function for or against risk of the decision-maker is at best of minor significance. However, for the evaluation of many projects the decision might well depend on the variance of the returns and the attitude towards risk.

---

[6] Expected utility is viewed here as the utility assigned to a certain probability distribution of income. (This concept merely implies that preferences can be expressed in the sense described by von Neumann and Morgenstern and does not require measurability of utility). Since only the variance of total income approaches zero, the compensation principle requires income to be additive, regardless from which project it is derived, or in other words, the utility of income must be the same regardless of where the income is earned.

[7] Some of this kind of variability of outcome can be adequately reflected in calculating expected returns and does not need to be analyzed in terms of subjective preferences. For instance, a sugar project which is designed to supply the raw material for a factory with a fixed capacity will yield a smaller expected return if sugar yields vary greatly from year to year than if yields are stable, since higher than normal yields cannot be processed and, hence, do not compensate for lower than normal yields.

A more specific use of gathering risk information (based on *a priori* or subjective probabilities) is for evaluating activities designed to eliminate or reduce the chances of unfavorable results. One such activity might be the gathering of more information, another the timing of investments or scheduling of various activities, and still another is the specific consideration of sequentially related outcomes. Much research is currently under way on all of these problems in the operations research and decision theory fields and a comprehensive review would be beyond the scope of this report. However, by way of some simple illustrations, we may gain some appreciation of the kind of problems and methods of solutions suggested by these theories.

Value of information

Consider first a simple problem in which we ask whether or not an investment should be held up until further information can be gathered. Basically, this is an expected benefit-cost analysis of the information gathering activity, where the expected benefits are determined on the basis of an *a priori* estimated probability function. What are the expected benefits? Assume that a project has been appraised in terms of a probability distribution of

FIGURE 3

PROBABILITY DISTRIBUTION OF PRESENT VALUE, *R*

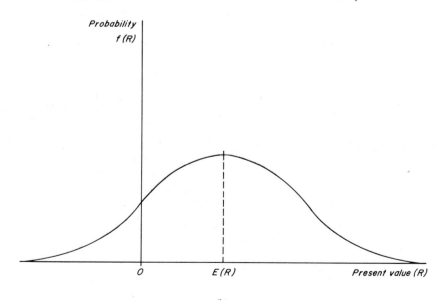

the present value of net benefits as outlined in Chapter III, and graphically shown in Figure 3. Now assume that on the basis of this probability distribution, the decision would be to go ahead with the investment. Assume furthermore, that a consultants' firm suggests to us that for a (probably high) cost, C, it can gather sufficient intelligence to tell us in fact precisely (highly unlikely!) what the present value from this investment will be. If the precise estimate turns out to be greater than 0, we would still go ahead with the investment and the gain from having employed the consultants' firm would be zero. If, however, the precise estimate of the present value, R_1 turns out to be less than zero, we would not undertake the investment and we would be spared a loss thanks to the consultants. On the basis of the probability distribution, $f(R)$, the expected benefit of the information gathering activity (avoidance of losses due to the wrong decision) would equal the weighted area under the probability curve to the left of $R = 0$, or

$$\text{Expected benefit}[8] = \int_{\infty}^{0} f(R) \ R \ dR \tag{3}$$

If indeed we believed that the consultants can give us a more precise estimate, we would employ them only if the expected benefits exceed their costs. Of course, it is quite likely that the gathering of additional information activity will take time, which is then an additional cost item to be taken into consideration.

For another example, consider that our organization is quite conservative in its attitude towards risk and that on the basis of the same probability distribution presented in Figure 3 the decision would have been not to go ahead with the investment. It is intuitively clear that the expected value of getting a precise (certain) estimate of the present value of net benefits is greater for this organization than in the first case. The expected benefits of the information gathering activity (avoidance of missing the opportunity for a profit due to the wrong decision) equals now the weighted area under the probability curve to the right of $R = 0$, i.e.

$$\text{Expected benefit} = \int_{0}^{\infty} f(R) \ R \ dR \tag{4}$$

From this simple illustration, it is seen that both the probability distribution and the organization's attitude towards risk (i.e. the decision function)

---

[8] The approximate benefits can be evaluated, of course, quite quickly by approximating the area under the probability distribution and neglecting the area to the left of some R which has an extremely small chance of occurrence. Furthermore, the probability distribution need not be, of course, a normal distribution.

would affect the value of additional information giving a precise and certain forecast of R. Usually, additional information will simply lead to a more precise, but still uncertain estimate. Hence, the formulae for expected benefit in this and the previous paragraph represent only the maximum (or most optimistic) estimates of the benefits from the information-gathering activity.

Alternative project strategies

More typically, project appraisal involves weighing of alternative strategies with respect to particular project aspects: how many roads are to be paved, how many bridges, how many farmers are to receive fertilizer, how much water per acre, etc. Once having made explicit how various elements interact to yield a measure of the economic or financial returns of the project, it is usually quite easy to calculate the project's performance with alternative strategies. Consider, for instance, the probability distributions of the present value of net benefits with project alternatives (A), (B) and (C) shown in Figure 4. In (B) and (C) project coverage has been reduced

FIGURE 4
PROBABILITY DISTRIBUTIONS OF PRESENT VALUE FOR
ALTERNATIVE PROJECT STRATEGIES

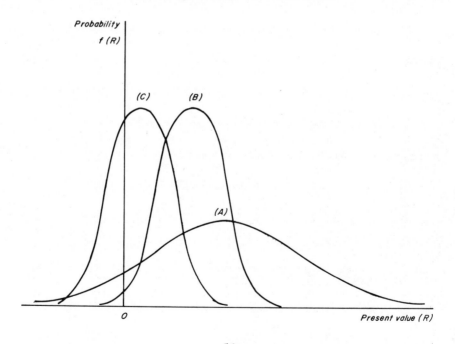

to exclude primarily some activities with highly uncertain results. Project proposal (A) includes all activities. If we were very unwilling to take a chance of getting a negative result, project alternative (B) may be more attractive than (A) in spite of a lower expected (mean) present value. However, alternative (C) may be ruled out completely because not only is the mean present value lower than for (A) and (B), but also the chances for getting a negative present value are higher than for (A) and (B).

Time related problems

Another specific application of the probabilistic approach is to time related problems, that is, where the results of a particular course of action in one period depend on uncertain events in another period, or when a future course of action will be determined by the realization of an uncertain event in an earlier period. Such problems particularly arise in planning of optimum storage facilities. Related to this, though somewhat different, is the general problem of sequential scheduling of investments when future benefits are uncertain.

The problem can be illustrated by the following highly simplified example. Suppose that the object is to build a grain storage facility and we wish to compare the expected net benefits. The benefits from having a storage facility will depend, of course, on the size of the grain harvest in a particular year (which in turn may be largely determined by climatic conditions). Let us assume that the probability distribution of the amount of storable grain is:

Probability	Amount of Grain for Storage
1/3	2
1/3	1
1/3	0

That is, in some years grain production will be too low to leave any surpluses to store. To simplify the problem, assume that the planning horizon is only two periods and for some reason the grain can be sold only at the end of the two periods. First, we wish to determine the expected amount of grain stored for different sizes of storehouses, since the storage capacity and the supply of grain determine the expected amount of grain stored.

The potential amounts of grain for storage can be determined by observing the "probability tree" where each branch has a probability of 1/3 (in our case) in the first year and $(1/3)^2 = 1/9$ in the second year. The numbers in circles are the potential cumulative amounts of grain for storage.

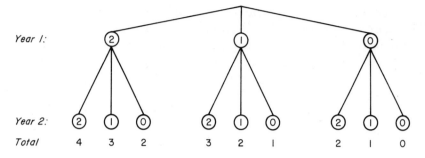

Year 1:

Year 2:

Total

| | 4 | 3 | 2 | | 3 | 2 | 1 | | 2 | 1 | 0 |

The expected storable grain is, of course:

$$\left(\frac{1}{9}\right)4 + \left(\frac{2}{9}\right)3 + \left(\frac{3}{9}\right)2 + \left(\frac{2}{9}\right)1 + \left(\frac{1}{9}\right)0 = 2$$

If the storage capacity is 2, the amount of grain stored could never exceed 2, hence the expected amount of grain in store is:

$$\left(\frac{6}{9}\right)2 + \left(\frac{2}{9}\right)1 + \left(\frac{1}{9}\right)0 = \frac{14}{9}$$

Similarly, if the storage capacity is 3, the expected amount of grain in store is:

$$\left(\frac{3}{9}\right)3 + \left(\frac{3}{9}\right)2 + \left(\frac{2}{9}\right)1 + \left(\frac{1}{9}\right)0 = \frac{17}{9}$$

Obviously, a storage capacity of 4 would be sufficient to accommodate all the expected grain available for storage, i.e. 2. To determine the storage capacity which maximizes expected net benefits, one would then merely have to know the value per unit of grain stored and subtract the cost (including interest charges) of each storehouse, respectively, from its expected revenue. One further consideration could then be the variability of benefits, which is not the same for the two storage operations.

In addition, however, we could also investigate a sequential decision strategy, whereby we would initially build a storage capacity not to exceed the first year's potential storable grain. Depending on how much grain was actually stored in the first year we could subsequently add an additional storage capacity. For instance, one strategy might be to build initially a storage capacity of 1 and add another 1 if this storehouse fills up in the first year. The expected amount of grain stored is then:

$$\frac{2 + 2 + 1 + 2 + 2 + 1 + 1 + 1 + 0}{9} = \frac{12}{9}$$

Similarly, one could build an initial capacity of 2 and another 1 only if the storehouse fills up in the first year. The expected amount of stored grain would then be:

$$\frac{3 + 3 + 2 + 2 + 1 + 2 + 1 + 0}{9} = \frac{16}{9}$$

These sequential decision strategies must then be evaluated in terms of costs to determine the course of action which maximizes expected net benefits and the most desirable distribution of benefits.

Actual problems involve, of course, much more complicated decision environments with many more combinations of outcomes and actions to be considered. Nevertheless, sometimes first crude approximations of optimum solutions can be obtained by rather simple techniques. More precise solutions can be attained by using the dynamic programming technique.[9] Another solution technique recently applied to such problems, after the problem has been properly conceptualized, is computer simulation.[10]

---

[9] For dynamic programming see: R. E. Bellman, *Applied Dynamic Programming*, Princeton University Press, 1962, and O. R. Burt and D. R. Allison, "Farm Management Decisions with Dynamic Programming," *Journal of Farm Economics*, 1963, 45:121–136.

[10] For simulation methods see: P. Zusman and A. Amiad, "Farm Planning under Weather Uncertainty," *Journal of Farm Economics*, 1965, 47:574–594, and G. H. Orcutt, "Simulation of Economic Systems," *American Economic Review*, 1961, 50:893–907.

PART II

CASE ILLUSTRATIONS

V

CONSTRUCTION OF APPRAISAL MODELS
AND THEIR DEPLOYMENT

Any quantitative appraisal of a project, be it in a probability sense as advocated in Part I or otherwise, requires the construction of a model. A concise statement of the model is a prerequisite for a probability appraisal whether performed analytically or by simulation with a computer. This chapter briefly describes how one goes about constructing a formal project appraisal model, and the usefulness of such models for purposes beyond probability appraisal, particularly if the models have been programmed for computerized calculations.

Model Construction

Any project generates many types of costs and benefits. An appraisal cannot take all of them into account nor can the actual costs and benefits actually be observed. Hence, cost-benefit analysis is simply the construction of a model which captures anticipated major occurrences and analyzes them. Possible shortcomings of present appraisal procedures are not necessarily the result of inadequate models used in appraisals. Some models may be gross abstractions of what actually is likely to happen during the course of a project, yet may be the best ones feasible in the light of the available information and the appraisal objectives.

The difficulty with most currently used models in project appraisal is that they are often not clearly or fully stated. Component parts of the model are scattered throughout an appraisal report, while it has become standard procedure to show the "superstructure" of the model in the form of an annex table, listing annual costs and benefits and the internal rate of return estimate. It is usually difficult to find out how these costs and benefits are estimated and on the basis of what assumptions. It is as if an architect presented a maquette and, separately, a shopping bag filled with models of doors, windows, ornaments, etc. to a panel of judges charged with assessing a proposed building. Obviously, the judging would be very difficult and the effect on the final result of making small changes in the components of the building could not be easily ascertained.

A mathematical model as used in the context of this paper is merely a precise statement of the logic and the basic premises or assumptions used in appraising a project. Such a model does not require accurate quantitative information, nor does its deployment guarantee accurate quantitative estimates. The following illustrations are intended to illustrate the technique for constructing a mathematical model.

A project model can be extremely crude and simple or very refined and complex. An extremely crude model would be a statement that, to determine the internal rate of return it is necessary to find the rate, r, which makes the prescribed number of discounted net benefits sum up to zero. Or in algebraic notation:[1]

Choose r such that

$$\sum \left[(1 + r)^{-t} \times \text{Net Benefit}_t\right] = 0 \qquad (1)$$

where $t = 1, 2, \ldots, \mathbf{n}$

This project appraisal model would then consist of an explicit listing of $\mathbf{n}$ annual net benefits (negative or positive) and their relationship to an internal rate of return. This is obviously an extremely crude model. For a case in which no data on specific inputs or outputs or prices can be obtained, or for a project which is extremely small or similar to previously analyzed projects, this crude model may be the best possible one for the purpose.

The eight equations presented below constitute a model which expands the simple model consisting of equation (1) above, to show how annual costs and benefits are related to explicit projections of other variables. It is still not very specific on many assumptions likely to be made in the course of a project appraisal. However, it illustrates the kind of model which could

---

[1] Variables or parameters which are used as given data without specifying how they are estimated are shown in boldface.

be prepared in advance of specific appraisals for projects of a similar nature:

Choose r such that

$$\sum \left[(1 + r)^{-t} \times \text{Net Benefit}_t \right] = 0 \tag{1}$$

where $t = 1, 2, \ldots, n$

In this equation net benefits are no longer given data, but are derived from other, more basic data, as described in the following 7 equations.

$$\text{Net Benefit}_t = \text{Revenue}_t - \text{Cost}_t \tag{2}$$

$$\text{Cost}_t \begin{cases} = k_t \times \text{Project Cost when } t \leq c \\ = \text{Maintenance Cost when } t > c \end{cases} \tag{3}$$

$$\text{Project Cost} = \text{Structures} + \text{Consultants} + \text{Administration} \tag{4}$$

$$\text{Structures} = \text{Quantity} \times \text{Price S} \tag{5}$$

$$\text{Revenue}_t \begin{cases} = 0 & \text{when} \quad t \leq c \\ = ((t - c)/f) \\ \quad \times \text{Full Development Revenue when } c < t < (c + f) \\ = \text{Full Development Revenue} \quad \text{when} \quad t \geq (c + f) \end{cases} \tag{6}$$

$$\text{Full Development Revenue} = \text{Output} \times \text{Price O} \tag{7}$$

$$\text{Output} = \text{Output per Firm} \times \text{Number of Firms} \tag{8}$$

Equation (3) simply states that during the construction period c, the cost is some proportion, k_t, of the total project cost, and thereafter the cost is a constant maintenance cost. Equation (4) states that the project cost is derived from estimates of three distinct types, say, structures, consultants' fees and administrative cost. Equation (5) states that the cost of structures is based on estimates of the number of structures needed and their per unit cost. Equation (6) states that annual revenue is zero during the construction period, c; increases at a constant rate, f, during the development period, and remains constant from there on. Equation (7) states that revenue at full development is the total output times per unit price and equation (8) states that the output is estimated from the output per typical firm and the number of firms participating in the project.

The purpose here is simply to show what is involved in preparing a formal statement of a model. Clearly, it is nothing but a concise statement of how a project is being appraised. The use of mathematical language certainly presumes nothing about the preciseness of the quantitative estimates used in the appraisal. It merely codifies the logic used in going about the appraisal. For this reason, no unusual mathematical skills are required to construct such a model. In the case of the above eight-equation model, data would need to be provided for the following items:

n, the life of the project
k_i, the proportion of project cost incurred in each year during the construction period
c, the length of the construction period
Consultants, the cost of consultants
Administration, the cost of administration
Quantity, the number of structures
Price S, the price per structure
f, the development period (time between end of construction and attaining full development revenue)
Price O, the price per unit of output
Output per Firm, the output per average firm
Number of Firms, the number of participating firms

Deployment of Formal Models

Transcribing a model into a number of concise statements may be useful simply because this process reduces the likelihood of oversights. It may even turn out that after having invested in the adoption of formalized models, the users will find that the models speed up appraisals and make it easier and less time-consuming for persons who have not been involved in the appraisal to give critical judgments. However, the most important reason for preparing a mathematical model is that it provides an opportunity to subject a project to a much more adequate appraisal than would be otherwise possible. This advantage obtains because a mathematical model's deployment is uniquely adapted to calculations on high-speed computers.

Preparation of the project models, data collection, and determination of the uses to be made of the model are, of course, the sole responsibility of the experts: the engineers, the agronomists, the economists, etc. However, many of the advantages to be obtained from formalizing models derive from the ready availability of computers. With competent programmers to assist, the model deployment suggestions detailed below should not present any serious technical difficulties.

Once a formal model has been prepared it is likely to be used for various purposes.

Sensitivity analysis

Sensitivity analysis is essentially an investigation of how and to what extent individual factors and parameters are likely to influence the benefits derived from a project. Knowledge of sensitivity can affect project planning decisions and appraisal in several ways.

First of all, there are the many factors and parameters which influence the success or failure of a project and hence its merits, but which are outside of the control of project design or management. Clearly, the quantitative values of these factors and parameters cannot be known precisely. However, a sensitivity analysis prior to the detailed appraisal of the project can determine the relative value of information to be obtained from additional investigations. Furthermore, when additional precision of estimates cannot be attained, sensitivity analysis, combined with rough estimates of the extent of uncertainty about various factors and parameters, can provide a preliminary estimate of the risk that the rate of return will be lower than anticipated.

Equally important, sensitivity analysis makes it feasible to explore the benefits or costs of many alternative project designs and management features. Using the formulated model, one could quickly determine by how much a smaller project, a delay in construction, or alternate management features would affect the rate of return of the project. When costs and benefits of alternative design features are not known, it could at least be determined whether additional investigations are worthwhile.

Risk appraisal

As this paper will have already suggested, another important use of a simulation model is in estimating the risk or uncertainty involved in a project. Given a simulation model it is no longer necessary to base decisions on one projected value of a project's benefits derived from single valued projections of the many variables and parameters used in the evaluation. Instead we can utilize the more realistic projection of probability distributions for each of the variables and parameters and transform these into a probability distribution of the benefit derived from the project.

Risk appraisal by simulation can utilize information on the relative likelihood of realizing different values for each of the important variables and convert them into a probability distribution of the project's rate of return. The computer can be instructed to pick at random a value for each of the variables in accordance with its likelihood to occur. Based on one set of values for each of the variables, a rate of return is calculated. This process, if repeated say 200 or 300 times, results in a frequency distribution of the rate of return consistent with the assumed probability distributions of the relevant variables and parameters.

Feasibility appraisal with general models

To the extent that there are similarities in the way projects of the same type are appraised, it is useful to have a general model on hand prior to specific appraisals. This is similar to a statement, obvious one would suppose, that one ought to approach any such project appraisal with fairly detailed terms of reference. Clearly, some parts of the model might not be usable in all projects, because either they are not relevant, or the necessary data are lacking.

In other cases it may make sense to augment the model and make further refinements. Naturally, during the appraisal some components of costs or benefits may need to be estimated in other than the usual ways. This applies to technical as well as economic parameters. At this stage, then, it is desirable to graft onto the general model a number of equations describing the appraisal logic used in the particular case.

Ex-post evaluation

Finally, a formal statement of models is extremely useful for follow-up evaluations of projects. Explicit statements about the variables and parameters assumed to influence the appraisal and their assumed values will facilitate the collection of useful data for testing appraisal practices. Sensitivity analyses and risk appraisal performed during the appraisal can provide the basis for identifying the more important variables to be kept under continuous surveillance. As actually realized values become available, the model can be modified to make repeated quick recalculations of the actual benefits.

A project may turn out better than, worse than, or about the same as anticipated without the credit or blame being attributable to the appraisal, as Hirschman has shown.[2] Hence, useful lessons are more likely to be learned if we concentrate on revaluating our predictions about specific factors and how they relate to the overall success of projects, rather than if we limit our attention to the success or failure of individual projects.

---

[2] A. O. Hirschman, *Development Projects Observed*, The Brookings Institution, Washington, D.C., 1967.

VI

CASE ILLUSTRATION –
A HIGHWAY PROJECT

The Model

The highway project appraisal model presented below is an example of how rate of return calculations normally performed in appraising highway improvement projects can be presented as a formal model statement. The model and data used below for illustrating application of appraisal methods under uncertainty closely approximate the model and data used in a pre-appraisal of an actual project.[1] The project calls for paving (laying and surfacing) a 64-mile long road. The project is supposed to be completed in two years. The major measurable benefits consist of road user savings and road maintenance cost savings. The extent of these benefits depends a great deal on the estimated traffic volume. The road may result in some induced traffic, but for the purposes of our illustration we will neglect this kind of benefit.

A conventional project appraisal report would give a table like Table 9. The costs and benefits shown in this table are based on best estimates of various items affecting the project costs and benefits. The assumptions on

---

[1] The subsequent presentation is not to be regarded as a case study. The data and the analyses are merely hypothetical illustrations of some decision environments in which the methods discussed in this paper might serve a useful function.

which these estimates are based may be spelled out in other tables or in the text of the report; very often they are not explicitly recorded.

To introduce more or less formal model construction and simulation into the presentation, one simply writes out explicitly in algebraic form the model used for measuring the rate of return (Table 11). To construct this model, one does more or less what one would do in finding the best route on a road map. On the map, one locates the desired final destination, identifies the best road leading to it, and then working back from road to road, plots a route back to the point of origin. In taking the actual trip, one starts, of course, with the road nearest to one's origin. Similarly, in constructing an appraisal model, one identifies the final objective, working backwards through intermediate objectives to the data requirement. When instructing a computer or a statistical clerk we must naturally proceed in the opposite direction, starting with the very basic input data and calculating with each equation new data which then become further input data. If one wants to follow the logic of a model constructed for computer calculations, it is a good idea to start at the end and read backwards.

The flow chart is a visual aid, giving a bird's eye view of the model (see Figure 5). Each box represents a sub-model which could be deleted or modified to suit particular circumstances. Further sub-models could also be added on. For instance, if project costs could vary a great deal with findings from future soil testing, a model might be added on to reflect this relationship.

Table 12 summarizes the data used for this exercise. The second column in Table 12 describes the variable, and the third the best (single point) estimate of its value. The first column gives the equation number in Table 11 in which the variable is used. These single valued variables are those used in the original appraisal before resorting to probability analysis. Ignoring column 4 for the moment, the values shown in the third column would exactly reproduce the costs and benefits and rate of return shown in Table 9.

It should be noted that the model is actually more general than necessary for this specific project, since there are no benefits from reduction in length of road in this case. This, of course, in no way interfers with the use of the model. When no **Reduction Miles** figures are given, the statistical clerk or computer simply assumes a value of zero and carries out the calculations of benefits attributing zero benefits due to reduction in miles. On the other hand, the model is far from general enough to handle all road appraisals. For instance, benefits from generated new traffic are not included. But it is easy to see how a series of equations could be added to handle these calculations. In practice, one could either have a very general model utiliz-

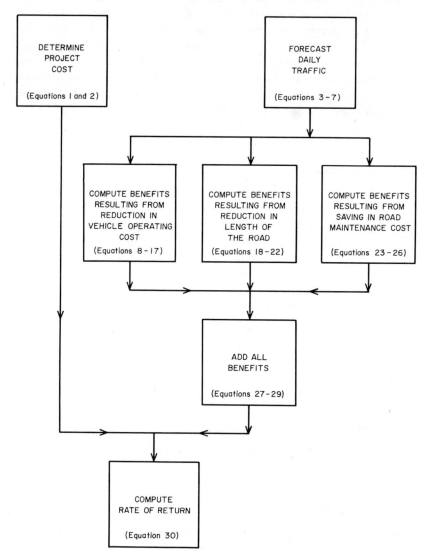

FIGURE 5
FLOW CHART FOR ROAD PROJECT APPRAISAL

ing only the equations for which variables have non-zero values, or one could prepare in advance a series of sub-models or "packages" which would be put together in each case according to the nature of the project.

We have shown in Chapter V that there are three basic ways in which simulation of a model as presented here can improve the appraisal of a project. First, it makes it more feasible to ask how changes in the project would affect the rate of return; if they are advantageous, one would proceed to improve the project plan. Second, one can find out whether it is worthwhile to collect more information and what information should be sought. Third, one can determine by how much the rate of return would be different if other than the best estimates for its more important determinants were to materialize, and what the probability is of getting a rate of return in a specified range.

Sensitivity Analysis

Advantages of a postponement

As an illustration of how a change in the project plan could affect the rate of return, let us consider a three-year postponement of project initiation. Assuming no changes in costs, we would expect the road investment, if delayed, to yield a higher return, since traffic is expected to grow. But by how much? The answer given with the aid of the model, is that the rate of return would be 14.3 percent instead of 11.6 percent.

The value of more information

A policy question we may need to investigate is whether we should gather further information. In deriving the estimates presented in Table 9 we have had to make a very rough guess about the current (or initial) traffic level. Let us now suppose that at some cost it is possible to get information on the exact level of initial traffic. What is the value of that information? It is possible to put a value on this information, so we may decide whether it should be obtained, in the following way:

(a) Evaluate the probabilities of finding various levels of initial traffic.

(b) Calculate the present value of the road investment for various levels of initial traffic, given a discount rate which reflects the opportunity cost of capital.

(c) Determine whether without further information, the decision would be to go ahead with the project or not.

(d) Calculate the expected value of the additional information as the sum of the negative present values obtained in (b) times their probabilities, if the decision without additional information was to go ahead, and as the sum of the positive present values obtained in (b)

TABLE 9: Highway Project Benefits and Costs, Single Valued Estimates

('000 units)

Year	Project Costs	Vehicle Operating Cost Saving	Road Maintenance Cost Saving	Net Benefits
		Benefits		
1	954			(−560)
2	954			(−560)
3		84	4	88
4		90	5	95
5		97	6	103
6		104	7	111
7		112	8	120
8		120	10	130
9		129	12	141
10		139	13	152
11		149	16	165
12		161	17	178
13		173	19	192
14		186	21	207
15		200	24	224
16		215	26	241
17		231	29	260
18		248	33	281
19		267	36	303
20		287	40	327
21		309	43	352
22		333	47	380

The internal rate of return is approximately 11.6%.

times their probabilities if this decision was to not continue the project.

Let us assume that opinions from different sources about the current level of traffic and our own interpretation of the facts lead us to think that initial traffic might be as shown in columns 1 through 5 in Table 10. For instance, we assume that there is a 5 percent chance that initial traffic is as low as 33 cars, 19 trucks, 5 buses and 11 trailers, but that there is a 20 percent chance that initial traffic consists of 39 cars, 22 trucks, 6 buses and 14 trailers. Let us further assume that the four traffic series are perfectly correlated, i.e. that if, in fact, car traffic turns out be 20 percent lower than the expected (average) level, then truck traffic will likewise be 20 percent less than expected. Column 6 in Table 10 gives the present value of benefits from the project for different initial traffic counts, assuming a 10 percent discount rate.

Let us now consider the benefits from hiring a consultant firm to ascer-

TABLE 10: **Probability Distribution of Initial Traffic Levels and Corresponding Present Value of Project Net Benefits**

Probability	Cars	Trucks	Buses	Trailers	Present Value (*units*)
		Initial Average Daily Traffic			
.05	33	19	5	11	−106,257
.05	35	20	5	12	−45,872
.10	37	21	5	13	14,514
.20	39	22	6	14	91,648
.20	41	23	6	15	152,033
.20	43	24	6	16	212,419
.10	45	25	5	17	256,057
.05	47	26	5	18	316,443
.05	49	27	5	19	376,828

tain the exact level of current traffic. To determine the benefits, we first ask what would happen without the additional information. If on the basis of currently available information the decision would be to implement the project, additional information would be beneficial only if it were to turn out that the initial traffic were so low as to result in a negative present value of benefits. Based on the probability distribution and the related present-value-of-benefits distribution stated in Table 10, there is only a 10 percent chance that the exact traffic count will turn up information which would change our original decision. The expected benefit of the additional information is the sum of the potential losses (negative present values of benefits) times their respective probabilities, i.e. $(.05) \times (-106,257) + (.05) \times (-45,872) = 7,606$ units.

If without additional information the decision would have been to shelve the project because we are not willing to take *any* chances of encountering losses, information on the exact traffic level would be beneficial if the traffic count would be high enough to justify the project. The value of this information is then the sum of the positive present value of benefits which would have been foregone without exact information, times the respective probabilities, i.e. $(.10) \times (14,514) + \ldots + (.05) \times (376,828) = 152,941$ units.

Variables beyond our control

As an illustration of sensitivity analysis about factors which affect the outcome of the project, but over which we cannot exercise any control, we may ask how lower rates of traffic growth than originally assumed would affect the projected rate of return. The answer is that a 20 percent reduction in the rates of traffic growth would reduce the rate of return from 11.6

to 9.7 percent. Similarly, a 20 percent reduction in the originally assumed levels of initial traffic would reduce the rate of return to 8.8 percent.

At present, the highway under consideration serves a special traffic of truck trailers in addition to normal traffic. This traffic is considered temporary until an alternative route opens up. Because of its temporary nature, this special traffic was initially disregarded in the rate of return calculations. Let us now ask how the presence of this special traffic affects the rate of return, assuming its average daily level will be 35 trailers until the fourth year of the project and will thereafter decline at the rate of 20 percent per year. The answer is that the rate of return would increase from 11.6 to 14.2 percent.

We have now conducted a series of what are called sensitivity analyses. We have seen that these analyses can be quite useful with respect to decisions over which we can exercise some measure of control, such as postponement of the project and obtaining further information about the initial daily traffic level. However, it is far from clear how to interpret the sensitivity analyses on variables which are beyond our control. Without making a judgment about the probability of getting 20 percent lower than projected traffic growth rates, and without knowing about the possibilities of realizing other than the projected values for other variables and how errors of projection compensate or compound the effects, there is little ground for judging the riskiness of the project. A much better insight can be gained by considering simultaneously the uncertainties of a group of variables.

Probability Distribution of Rate of Return

In risk analysis, the single point estimates (or best estimates) are first of all partially replaced by estimated probability distributions, when this is a more realistic assessment of the information available to the experts. The fourth column of Table 12 gives probability distributions which are similar to distributions which have been used in the actual case application of a risk analysis. The shapes of the distribution employed are illustrated in Figure 6 and their exact properties are described in many statistics textbooks.[2] Procedures for obtaining the collaboration of experts little accustomed to presenting probability information are discussed in a later paper in this series.[3]

---

[2] See for instance: A. M. Mood, *Introduction to the Theory of Statistics*, 1950, McGraw-Hill Corp. New York.

[3] L. Y. Pouliquen, *"Risk Analysis in Project Appraisal,"* World Bank Staff Occasional Paper No. 11.

FIGURE 6

GRAPHIC ILLUSTRATION OF TYPES OF PROBABILITY DISTRIBUTIONS
USED IN APPRAISAL OF HIGHWAY PROJECT

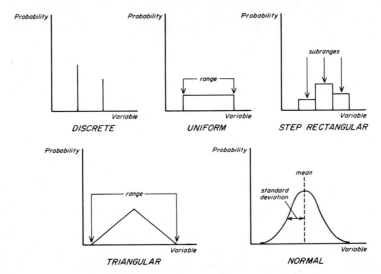

The rate of return analysis consists now of repeated rate-of-return calculations, each time utilizing a different set of values for each of the variables in the model subject to probability distributions. For deriving these sets of values the computer takes random readings on each variable with the chance of a value being selected determined by the variable's probability distribution. Figure 7 shows the cumulative, relative frequency distribution of the rate of return derived from a sample of 300 rate-of-return calculations. The expected (mean) rate of return of the project is 12.2 percent and the standard deviation of the rate of return is 3.3 The observed distribution fits fairly closely the theoretical normal probability distribution. Therefore, normal distribution tables can be used in this case for making statements on the extent to which uncertainties surrounding the project (special traffic, traffic growth rates, initial traffic, construction costs, road user savings, etc.) translate into uncertainties about the realizable rate of return. If interest were to focus primarily on an opportunity cost of capital of 10 percent, we could state on the basis of a considerable amount of analysis that the probability of realizing a rate of return of less than 10 percent is about 25 percent. We can also say that there is about a 3 percent chance that the rate of return will be less than 6 percent.

Summing up, sensitivity analyses on policy or controllable variables and probability appraisal can be expected to contribute new insights into the

FIGURE 7
CUMULATIVE PROBABILITY DISTRIBUTION OF RATE OF RETURN

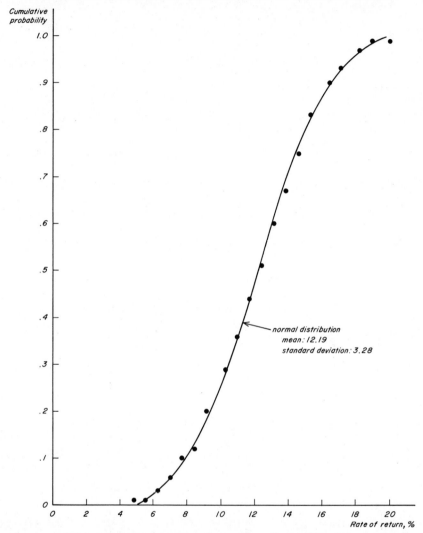

anatomy of the economic benefits of a project. It is difficult to generalize about the extent of this contribution. In any case consideration of alternative courses of action in a project is almost always useful. The value of knowing the estimated probability distribution depends on the credibility of the judgments made in the analysis and on knowledge of the probability distributions of alternative projects.

TABLE 11: Road Project Appraisal Model

1. (Project Cost) = (Pavement Base) + (Sub-Base/Shoulders) + (Earth Works) + (Borrow Materials) + (Others)

2. $(\text{Cost})_t = \begin{cases} \dfrac{(\text{Project Cost})}{(\text{Construction Time})} \, (n) & \text{if } t \leq (\text{Construction Time}) \\ C & \text{if } t > (\text{Construction Time}) \end{cases}$

3. $(\text{Traffic Cars})_t = (1 + \text{Traffic Growth Cars})^t \times (\text{Initial Traffic Cars})$
4. $(\text{Traffic Trucks})_t = (1 + \text{Traffic Growth Trucks})^t \times (\text{Initial Traffic Trucks})$
5. $(\text{Traffic Buses})_t = (1 + \text{Traffic Growth Buses})^t \times (\text{Initial Traffic Buses})$
6. $(\text{Traffic Trailers})_t = (1 + \text{Traffic Growth Trailers})^t \times (\text{Initial Traffic Trailers})$
7. $(\text{Traffic Special})_t = (1 + \text{Traffic Growth Special})^t \times (\text{Initial Traffic Special})$
8. (Cost Saving p.v.m. Car) = Cost p.v.m. Old Road Car − Cost p.v.m. New Road Car
9. (Cost Saving p.v.m. Truck) = Cost p.v.m. Old Road Truck − Cost p.v.m. New Road Truck
10. (Cost Saving p.v.m. Bus) = Cost p.v.m. Old Road Bus − Cost p.v.m. New Road Bus
11. (Cost Saving p.v.m. Trailer) = Cost p.v.m. Old Road Trailer − Cost p.v.m. New Road Trailer
12. (Cost Saving p.v.m. Special) = Cost p.v.m. Old Road Special − Cost p.v.m. New Road Special
13. $(\text{Operating Cost Saving Car})_t = (\text{Cost Saving Car})_t \times (\text{Traffic Cars})_t \times (\text{Miles})_t \times 365$
14. $(\text{Operating Cost Saving Truck})_t = (\text{Cost Saving Truck})_t \times (\text{Traffic Trucks})_t \times (\text{Miles})_t \times 365$
15. $(\text{Operating Cost Saving Bus})_t = (\text{Cost Saving Bus})_t \times (\text{Traffic Buses})_t \times (\text{Miles})_t \times 365$
16. $(\text{Operating Cost Saving Trailer})_t = (\text{Cost Saving Trailer})_t \times (\text{Traffic Trailer})_t \times (\text{Miles})_t \times 365$
17. $(\text{Operating Cost Saving Special})_t = (\text{Cost Saving Special})_t \times (\text{Traffic Special})_t \times (\text{Miles})_t \times 365$

Table 11, cont.

18. (Mileage Cost Saving Car)$_t$ = (Traffic Cars)$_t$ × (Cost Travel Old Road Car) × (**Reduction Miles**) × 365
19. (Mileage Cost Saving Truck)$_t$ = (Traffic Trucks) × (Cost Travel Old Road Truck) × (**Reduction Miles**) × 365
20. (Mileage Cost Saving Bus)$_t$ = (Traffic Buses) × (Cost Travel Old Road Bus) × (**Reduction Miles**) × 365
21. (Mileage Cost Saving Trailer)$_t$ = (Traffic Trailers) × (Cost Travel Old Road Trailer) × (**Reduction Miles**) × 365
22. (Mileage Cost Saving Special)$_t$ = (Traffic Special) × (Cost Travel Old Road Special) × (**Reduction Miles**) × 365
23. (Traffic Units)$_t$ = (Traffic Cars)$_t$ + 2(Traffic Trucks)$_t$ + 2(Traffic Buses)$_t$ + 3(Traffic Trailers)$_t$ + 3(Traffic Special)$_t$
24. (Maintenance Cost Old Road)$_t$ = **a** + **b** × (Traffic Units)$_t$, where a and b are constants
25. (Maintenance Cost New Road)$_t$ = **c** + **d** × (Traffic Units)$_t$, where c and d are constants
26. (Maintenance Cost Saving)$_t$ = (Maintenance Cost Old Road)$_t$ − (Maintenance Cost New Road)$_t$ × (**Miles**)
27. (Total Operating Cost Saving)$_t$ = (Operating Cost Saving Car)$_t$ + (Operating Cost Saving Truck)$_t$
   + (Operating Cost Saving Bus)$_t$ + (Operating Cost Saving Trailer)$_t$
   + (Operating Cost Saving Special)$_t$
28. (Total Mileage Cost Saving)$_t$ = (Mileage Cost Saving Car)$_t$ + (Mileage Cost Saving Truck)$_t$ + (Mileage Cost Saving Bus)$_t$
   + (Mileage Cost Saving Trailer)$_t$ + (Mileage Cost Saving Special)$_t$

29. (Benefits)$_t$ = $\Big\{$ (Total Operating Cost Saving)$_t$ = (Total Mileage Cost Savings)$_t$
   + (Maintenance Cost Saving) when $t >$ (Construction Time)
   C   when $t <$ (Construction Time)

30. Calculate r such that $\sum (1 + r)^{-t}$ (Cost)$_t$ = $\sum (1 + r)^{-t}$ (Benefits)$_t$, $t = 1, \ldots, \mathbf{n}$

Notes: Traffic refers to Average Daily Traffic; Cost p.v.m. is cost per vehicle mile; any variable followed by subscript t indicates amount per year. Given data is in **boldface**.

79

TABLE 12: Input Data for Road Project Appraisal

Equation	Item	Single Valued Estimate	Probability Distribution	
			Probability	**Cost**
1	Pavement Base	466,000	Discrete:	
			40%	579,000 (6" base)
			60%	466,000 (5" Base)
1	Sub-Base/Shoulders	311,150	Step Rectangular:	
			(i) If cost of base is 579,000 then:	
			Probability is	Cost Sub-base and Shoulders is
			30%	150,000–240,000
			50%	240,000–300,000
			20%	300,000–400,000
			(ii) If cost of base is 466,000 then:	
			Probability is	Cost Sub-base and Shoulders is
			30%	200,000–300,000
			50%	300,000–340,000
			20%	340,000–440,000
1	Earthworks	92,400	Uniform on range 46,200 and 92,400	
1	Borrow Materials	15,000	Triangular on range 10,000 to 30,000	
1	Others	1,023,000	Triangular on range 941,850 to 1,163,500	
2	Construction Time	2	Normal: Mean 41, Standard Deviation 3.35	
3	Initial Traffic Cars	41	Triangular on range 15 to 35	
4	Initial Traffic Trucks	23	Normal: Mean 6, Standard Deviation 1	
5	Initial Traffic Buses	6	Normal: Mean 15, Standard Deviation 3.3	
6	Initial Traffic Trailers	15	Probability	Traffic Level
7	Initial Traffic Special	nil	25%	35
			75%	nil

Table 12, cont.

Equation	Item	Single Valued Estimate	Probability Distribution
3	Traffic Growth Cars	6%	Uniform on range 4% to 8%
4	Traffic Growth Trucks	8%	Uniform on range 6% to 10%
5	Traffic Growth Buses	6%	Uniform on range 4% to 8%
6	Traffic Growth Trailers	8%	Uniform on range 6% to 10%. Growth of trucks and trailers are fully correlated
7	Traffic Growth Special Period 1968–1972 Period 1972 on	0 −20%	
8	Cost Travel Old Road Car	0.0613	Uniform on range −12% to +15%; all fully correlated.[a] In addition operating cost of trucks is varied uniformly on range −5% to +10% to account for uncertainty on size of trucks
9	Cost Travel Old Road Truck	0.1076	
10	Cost Travel Old Road Bus	0.1516	
11	Cost Travel Old Road Trailer	0.215	
12	Cost Travel Old Road Special	0.215	
8	Cost Travel New Road Car	0.0479	
9	Cost Travel New Road Truck	0.0670	
10	Cost Travel New Road Bus	0.1034	[b]
11	Cost Travel New Road Trailer	0.141	
12	Cost Travel New Road Special	0.140	
13–17	Miles	64	
18–22	Reduction in Miles		
24	a	417.0	Uniform on range 3 and 5
24	b	3.6	
25	c	600.0	Uniform on range 1 and 2.5
25	d	2.25	
30	m (life of project)	20	Triangular on range 12 to 25 years

[a] This distribution is artificial and is only geared at getting a correct distribution of the savings from the improvement of the road.
[b] Ignored because variation of savings is fully taken care of by variation of operating costs on old road.

81

VII

CASE ILLUSTRATION—
A HYPOTHETICAL IRRIGATION PROJECT

To illustrate the data requirements, the procedure and the resulting information which is involved in a quantitative appraisal of the uncertainty of returns, consider the following hypothetical case.[1] The project may be thought of as an irrigation project where the present value of the returns is a function of the cost of establishing a facility and n annual equal net returns thereafter. The annual net returns consist of revenues obtained from the increased production of three crops. Both the number of acres and the yield per acre of crop 1 largely depend on wages farmers can earn in an alternative employment. The price of commodity 2 is assumed to be negatively correlated with the output of crop 2 by the project. Prices of commodities 1 and 3 are not affected by the project's output. First, the model for calculating present value of benefits is presented. The same model would be used whether one does a conventional appraisal or a probability appraisal. It is merely a systematic, explicit statement of how one might go about estimating the outcome of a variable based on knowledge about certain parameters and other variables. Next are shown the probability distributions of parameters which cannot be predicted to have a specific value with certainty. Finally, the results of a conventional appraisal and a probability appraisal are presented and contrasted.

---

[1] This chapter was written as an illustration of the principles developed in Chapter III.

TABLE 13: The Model

(1)	Acres in production of crop 1 (A) are a function of wage in an alternative employment (W).	$(A) = 10 - (W)$
(2)	Yield per acre of crop 1 (Y) is a function of wage in alternative employment (W).	$(Y) = 10 - 2(W)$
(3)	Production of crop 1 (X_1) is acres (A) times yield (Y) and a random effect (e_1).	$(X_1) = (A)(Y) + (e_1)$
(4)	Gross revenue from crop 1 (S_1) is price (Z_1) times production (X_1).	$(S_1) = (Z_1)(X_1)$
(5)	Price of crop 2 (Z_2) is a function of slope coefficient (b), production of crop 2 (X_2) and a random effect (e_2).	$(Z_2) = 10 - (b)(X_2) + (e_2)$
(6)	Gross revenue from crop 2 (S_2) is price (Z_2) times production (X_2).	$(S_2) = (Z_2)(X_2)$
(7)	Gross revenue from crop 3 (S_3) is price (Z_3) times production (X_3).	$(S_3) = (Z_3)(X_3)$
(8)	Annual net benefit (B) is gross revenues (S_1, S_2 and S_3) less annual cost.	$(B) = (S_1) + (S_2) + (S_3) - 70$
(9)	The sum of the discounting factors ($\sum a^t$) is a function of the life of the investment (n).	$(\sum a^t) = \sum (1 + .08)^{-t}$ $t = 1, \ldots, n$
(10)	Present value (R) is a function of the sum of the discount factors ($\sum a^t$) and the annual benefits (B), less the initial investment (B_1).[a]	$(R) = (\sum a^t)(B) - (B_1)$

[a] The discount rate used in the subsequent hypothetical calculation is 8 percent. For internal rate of return calculations, the equation is $0 = -(B_1) + \sum (1 + r)^{-t} (B)$ and r is the variable to be derived.

Probability Distribution of the Inputs

The 10 inputs needed for estimating the model are: wage (W), prices (Z_1) and (Z_3), production (X_2) and (X_3), and the initial investment cost (B_1), the life of the investment (n) a price-output coefficient (b) and the two random effects (e_1) and (e_2). Let us now assume that the probability distributions of these inputs are believed to be as follows:

TABLE 14: Probability of Various Outcomes of Events

Inputs	Outcome	Probability	Inputs	Outcome	Probability
W ($)	1	.30	B_1 ($)	1,600	.25
	2	.40		2,000	.50
	3	.30		2,400	.25
Z_1 ($)	2.4	.33	n (years)	5	.33
	3.0	.33		10	.33
	3.6	.33		15	.33
Z_3 ($)	3.5	.20	b	.06	.30
	5.0	.60		.10	.40
	6.5	.20		.14	.30
X_2 (tons)	30	.33	e_1 (tons)	-10	.30
	50	.33		0	.40
	70	.33		+10	.30
X_3 (tons)	14	.33	e_2 ($)	-0.4	.30
	20	.33		0	.40
	26	.33		0.4	.30

83

Conventional Appraisal of Present Value of Benefits

The conventional procedure for estimating the present value of the benefits (or alternatively the internal rate of return) is to use best estimates of the inputs and to calculate in sequence each of the 10 equations in the model. Alternatively, to be on the safe side, one may use conservative estimates for the inputs in the cost-benefit calculations.

The conventional appraisal procedure would have resulted in an estimate of the present value of the discounted benefits of $845 (or a rate of return of about 16 percent) assuming the means of the probability distributions of the inputs represent their best estimates. Assuming conservative estimates for each of the inputs are represented by 10 percent decreases in inputs Z_1, Z_3, X_2, X_3 and n, 10 percent increases in W, B and b, -5 for e_1 and $-.2$ for e_2, the present value would have been estimated as $-$114 (or a rate of return of about 6.5 percent). Next we see how these estimates compare with estimates obtained by probability analysis.

Appraisal by Probability Analysis

The same model and input distributions were used to derive a simulated distribution of present value and the internal rate of return.[2] The dots in Figures 8 and 9 represent relative frequencies of present value and internal rate of return estimates, respectively, based on 200 random sets of drawing from the input distributions. The resulting distributions are, of course, specific to the particular sample of 200 sets of drawings, though it is generally assumed that with large enough samples, chances are high that the

FIGURE 8
SIMULATED PROBABILITY DISTRIBUTION OF PRESENT VALUE

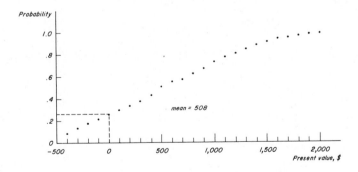

---

[2] The calculations were performed on a computer by courtesy of McKinsey & Company, Inc., utilizing their general program for risk analysis.

FIGURE 9
SIMULATED PROBABILITY DISTRIBUTION OF
INTERNAL RATE OF RETURN

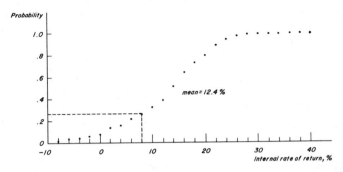

sample distribution nearly approximates the "true" distribution. Note-worthy is the fact that the expected (mean) presented value is $508, and considerably less than estimated by the conventional analysis.[3] Similarly, the mean internal rate of return is 12.4 percent as compared with almost 16 percent by conventional analysis. It is, of course, also easy to give conservative estimates by merely glancing at the figures. For instance, chances of getting less than a present value of zero, or correspondingly, a rate of return of 8 percent is about 26 percent. Using a full probability appraisal, it is clearly possible to derive conservative estimates which have a well-defined interpretation and can be evaluated in terms of alternatives. By comparison, the conventional conservative estimate is not a clearly defined entity in terms of the final benefit-cost measure.

---

[3] The exact mean present value solving the model by applying mathematical expectations is $574. The difference in the mean present value when calculated conventionally and by probability appraisal is entirely due to non-linear functional relations.

85

ANNEX

REVIEW OF SOME BASIC CONCEPTS AND RULES FROM PROBABILITY CALCULUS WITH SPECIFIC APPLICATIONS

The concepts and rules discussed briefly in this annex should be primarily useful for deriving the mean and variance of a variable which is a function of two or more other variables measured in terms of their probability distributions.[1] The presentation aims at providing a handy reference, not at mathematical rigor.

Some basic probability concepts

The problem-solving procedures for measuring the mean and variance of the present value of a stream of benefits from a project are specific applications of a few general rules from the probability calculus. Hence, a brief review of a few general rules are given below.[2]

---

[1] As a useful reference, in terms of more mathematical rigor yet brief presentation, the reader may consult R. V. Hogg and A. T. Craig, *Introduction to Mathematical Statistics*, Chapter 1 for probability and mathematical expectations concepts, and B. Wagle, "A Statistical Analysis of Risk in Capital Investment Projects," *Operations Research Quarterly*, Vol. 18, No. 1 for special applications in risk appraisal. See also F. S. Hillier, "The Derivation of Probabilistic Information for the Evaluation of Risky Investments," *Management Science*, Vol. 9, 1963.

[2] For simplicity of representation, we shall discuss here only discrete probability distribution.

First, let us define a probability distribution. Let all possible outcomes of an event be denoted by x_i, $i = 1 \ldots n$, and let the probabilities of each outcome be denoted by p_i, i.e.

$$f(x_i) = p_i$$

then $f(X)$ is a probability distribution if

$$\sum p_i = 1$$

and $\hspace{6cm} (i = 1, \ldots, n)$

$$p_i \geq 0$$

In words, the probabilities must sum to one and negative probabilities are not admissible.

The concept of probability distribution can be generalized to two or more variables. Let x_i and y_j be the outcomes of two events, and let the probability of each joint outcome x_i, y_j be denoted by p_{ij}, i.e.

$$f(x_i, y_j) = p_{ij} \hspace{1cm} (i = 1, \ldots, n, j = 1, \ldots, m)$$

then $f(X, Y)$ is a probability distribution if

$$\sum p_{ij} = 1$$

and $\hspace{4cm} (i = 1, \ldots, n, j = 1, \ldots, m)$

$$p_{ij} \geq 0$$

Mathematical expectations

One of the more useful concepts in problems involving probability distributions is that of a mathematical expectation. Let X be a set of events with a properly defined probability distribution $f(X)$ and let $g(X)$ be any function of X, then the mathematical expectation E (or the expected value) of $g(X)$ is:

$$E[g(X)] = \sum p_i\, g(x_i) \hspace{1cm} (i = 1, \ldots, n)$$

For instance, if $g(X) = X$, then,

$$E(X) = \sum p_i x_i \hspace{1cm} (i = 1, \ldots, n)$$

if $g(X) = X^2$, then

$$E(X^2) = \sum p_i x_i^2 \hspace{1cm} (i = 1, \ldots, n)$$

or if $g(X) = (X + 4)$, then

$$E(X + 4) = \sum p_i(x_i + 4) \hspace{1cm} (i = 1, \ldots, n)$$

The concept of mathematical expectations generalizes to two or more variables. Let X and Y be sets of events with a properly defined probability distribution, and let $g(X, Y)$ be any function of X and Y, then the expectation of $g(X, Y)$ is:

$$E[g(X, Y)] = \sum\sum p_{ij}\, g(x_i, y_j)$$
$$(i = 1, \ldots, n, j = 1, \ldots, m)$$

For instance $E(XY)$ is then,

$$E(XY) = \sum\sum p_{ij}\, x_i y_j \qquad (i = 1, \ldots, n, j = 1, \ldots, m)$$

Properties of mathematical expectations

Note the following properties of mathematical expectations:

(a) If k is a constant,

$$E(k) = k$$
$$\text{(since } E(k) = \sum p_i k$$
$$= k \sum p_i, \text{ and } \sum p_i = 1\text{)}$$

(b) If k is a constant and X is a variable,

$$E(kX) = k\, E(X)$$
$$\text{(since } E(kX) = \sum p_i k x_i = k \sum p_i x_i\text{)}$$

(c) If k_1 and k_2 are constants and X_1 and X_2 are variables

$$E(k_1 X_1 + k_2 x_2) = k_1\, E(X_1) + k_2\, E(X_2)$$

Special mathematical expectations

Some frequently used mathematical expectations are:

(A) *The mean:* $E(X)$

$$E(X) = \sum p_i x_i$$

(B) *The variance:* $V(X) = E(X - E(X))^2$

$$V(X) = \sum p_i\, (x_i - E(X))^2$$

The variance can be computed by the formula:[3]

$$E(X^2) - (E(X))^2 = \sum p_i x_i^2 - \left(\sum p_i x_i\right)^2$$

---

[3] The derivation is as follows:

$$E(X - E(X))^2 = E[X^2 - 2E(X)\, X + (E(X))^2]$$
$$= E(X^2) - 2(E(X))^2 + (E(X))^2$$
$$= E(X^2) - (E(X))^2$$

(C) *The covariance:*[4] cov. $(XY) = E(X - E(X))(Y - E(Y))$

$$\text{cov. } (XY) = \sum\sum p_{ij}(x_i - E(X))(y_i - E(Y))$$

Making use of the properties of expectations, it can be shown that the covariance is also

$$E(XY) - E(X)E(Y) = \sum\sum p_{ij}x_iy_j - \sum p_ix_i \sum p_jy_j$$

(D) *The mean of a linear function:*

If

$$Y = aX$$

then

$$E(Y) = aE(X)$$

(Note, therefore, that the mean of a linear function is a function of the mean. But the mean of a non-linear function is *not* a function of the mean, i.e. if $Y = aX^2$ then $E(Y) = aE(X^2)$ and $E(Y) \neq a(E(X))^2$

(E) *The variance of a linear function:*
Similarly,

$$V(Y) = a^2 V(X)$$

But if $Y = aX^2$, $V(Y) = a^2 V(X^2)$ and $V(Y) \neq a^2 (V(X))^2$

(F) *The mean of a sum:* $E(Y)$

Given that X_1 and X_2 are random variables and a_1 and a_2 are constants, such that $Y = a_1 X_1 + a_2 X_2$, the mean of the sum is

$$E(Y) = a_1 E(X_1) + a_2 E(X_2)$$

(G) *The variance of a sum:*[5] $V(Y)$

$$V(Y) = a_1{}^2 V(X_1) + a_2{}^2 V(X_2) + 2 a_1 a_2 \text{ cov. } (X_1 X_2)$$

---

[4] Also, cov. $(XY) = r V(X) V(Y)$, where r is the correlation coefficient.
[5] The variance of a sum can be derived as follows:
$$\begin{aligned} V(Y) &= E[a_1X_1 + a_2X_2 - a_1 E(X_1) - a_2 E(X_2)]^2 \\ &= E[a_1(X_1 - E(X_1)) + a_2(X_2 - E(X_2))]^2 \\ &= a^2 E(X_1 - E(X_1))^2 + a_2^2 E(X_1 - E(X_2))^2 \\ &\quad + 2a_1a_2 E[(X_1 - E(X))(X_2 - E(X_2))] \end{aligned}$$

(H) *The mean of a product* if the covariance is zero:
Note from (C) that if cov. $(XY) = 0$,

$$E(XY) = E(X) \, E(Y)$$

(I) *The variance of a product* if the covariance is zero:[6]

$$V(XY) = (E(X))^2 \, V(Y) + (E(Y))^2 \, V(X) + V(X) \, V(Y)$$

Special mathematical expectations useful in project appraisal

Assuming that the means of annual benefits are equal, let $a^t = (1 + r)^{-t}$; $t = 1, 2, \ldots, n$, $E(R)$ be the mean present value of a stream of benefits, and $E(X)$ be the mean benefit in each year, then,

$$E(R) = (a + a^2 + \ldots + a^n) \, E(X)$$

Assuming that the variance of annual benefits are equal, let $V(R)$ be the variance of the present value of a stream of benefits, $V(X)$ be the variance of the annual benefits, then if successive benefits are independent, i.e. all covariances are zero,

$$V(R) = (a^2 + a^4 + \ldots + a^{2n}) \, V(X)$$

if all successive benefits are perfectly correlated, i.e. cov. $(X_{ij}) = V(X)$ for $i, j = 1, 2, \ldots, n$, then,

$$V(R) = (a + a^2 + \ldots + a^n)^2 \, V(X)$$

---

[6] See L. A. Goodman, "On the Exact Variance of Products," *Journal of American Statistical Association*, 1960.

ANNEX TABLE 1: Mean of Present Value, by Year and Interest Rate

$$\sum (t\, a^t), t = 1, \ldots, n, \text{ where } a = (1 + r)^{-1}$$

Number of Years (n)	Rate of Interest (r)		
	6%	8%	10%
1	0.9434	0.9259	0.9091
2	2.7234	2.6405	2.5619
3	5.2422	5.0219	4.8158
4	8.4106	7.9619	7.5478
5	12.1471	11.3649	10.6523
6	16.3771	15.1461	14.0393
7	21.0328	19.2306	17.6317
8	26.0520	23.5530	21.3637
9	31.3791	28.0548	25.1806
10	36.9631	32.6868	29.0356
11	42.7579	37.4047	32.8911
12	48.7219	42.1699	36.7143
13	54.8163	46.9500	40.4804
14	61.0085	51.7170	44.1666
15	67.2680	56.4450	47.7576
16	73.5656	61.1154	51.2392
17	79.8794	65.7105	54.6018
18	86.1848	70.2141	57.8400
19	92.4643	74.6164	60.9465
20	98.7003	78.9064	63.9185

ANNEX TABLE 2: Variance of Present Value, by Year and Interest Rate

$$\sum a^{2t}, t = 1, \ldots, n, \text{ where } a = (1 + r)^{-1}$$

Number of Years (n)	Rate of Interest (r)		
	6%	8%	10%
1	.89000	.85734	.82645
2	1.68209	1.59237	1.50946
3	2.38705	2.22254	2.07393
4	3.01446	2.76281	2.54044
5	3.57285	3.22600	2.92598
6	4.06982	3.62311	3.24461
7	4.51212	3.96357	3.50794
8	4.90577	4.25546	3.72557
9	5.25611	4.50571	3.90543
10	5.56791	4.72026	4.05407
11	5.84542	4.90420	4.17692
12	6.09240	5.06190	4.27845
13	6.31221	5.19710	4.36236
14	6.50784	5.31301	4.43170
15	6.68195	5.41239	4.48901
16	6.83691	5.49759	4.53637
17	6.97482	5.57064	4.57551
18	7.09756	5.63326	4.60786
19	7.20680	5.68695	4.63459
20	7.30402	5.73298	4.65668
21	7.39055	5.77244	4.67494
22	7.46756	5.80627	4.69003
23	7.53610	5.83528	4.70250
24	7.59710	5.86015	4.71281
25	7.65139	5.88147	4.72133
26	7.69971	5.89975	4.72837
27	7.74271	5.91542	4.73419
28	7.78098	5.92886	4.73900
29	7.81504	5.94038	4.74297
30	7.84535	5.95026	4.74625

BIBLIOGRAPHY

Adelman, R. M. "Criteria for Capital Investment," *Operational Research Quarterly*, March 1965.

Arrow, K. J. "Alternative Approaches to the Theory of Choice in Risk-Taking Situations," *Econometrica*, Vol. 19, October 1951.

Arrow, K. J., T. Harris and J. Marshak. "Optimal Inventory Policy," *Econometrica*, Vol. 20, July 1951.

Bellman, R. *Adaptive Control Processes: A Guided Tour*. Princeton: Princeton University Press, 1961.

Burt, O. R. and D. R. Allison. "Farm Management Decisions with Dynamic Programming," *Journal of Farm Economics*, Vol. 45, 1963.

Dorfman, R. "Basic Economic and Technologic Concepts." Chapter in A. Maas et al., *Design of Water Resource Systems*. Cambridge: Harvard University Press, 1962.

Farrar, D. E. *The Investment Decision Under Uncertainty*. Englewood Cliffs, N.J.: Prentice-Hall, 1962.

Fellner, William. *Probability and Profit*. Homewood, Ill.: Richard D. Irwin, Inc., 1965.

Friedman, M. and L. T. Savage. "The Utility Analysis of Choice Involving Risk," *Journal of Political Economy*, Vol. 56, August 1948.

Goodman, L. A. "On the Exact Variance of Products," *Journal of American Statistical Association*, Vol. 55, 1960.

Hertz, O. B. "Risk Analysis in Capital Investment," *Harvard Business Review*, January–February 1964.

Hillier, F. S. "The Derivation of Probabilistic Information for the Evaluation of Risky Investments," *Management Science*, Vol. 9, 1963.

Hirshleifer, J. "Investment Decision Under Uncertainty: Applications of the State-Preference Approach," *The Quarterly Journal of Economics*, May 1966.

Hirshleifer, J. "Investment Decision Under Uncertainty: Choice-Theoretic Approaches," *The Quarterly Journal of Economics*, Vol. 79, November 1965.

Howard, R. A. "Dynamic Inference," *Operations Research*, Vol. 13, September 1965.

Lamberton, D. M. *The Theory of Profit*. Oxford: Basil Blackwell & Mott, Ltd., 1965.

Maas, A. *Design of Water Resource Systems*. Cambridge: Harvard University Press, 1962.

Markowitz, H. *Portfolio Selection: Efficient Diversification of Investments*. New York: John Wiley & Sons, 1954.

Marshak, J. "Money and the Theory of Assets," *Econometrica*, Vol. 6, 1938.

Masse, Pierre. *Optimal Investment Decisions*, Englewood Cliffs, N.J.: Prentice-Hall, 1962.

Modigliani, F. and K. J. Cohen. "The Significance and Uses of Ex Ante Data." Chapter IV in *Expectations, Uncertainty and Business Behavior*, edited by M. J. Bowman. New York: Social Science Research Council, 1958.

Orcutt, G. H. "Simulation of Economic Systems," *American Economic Review*, Vol. 50, 1961.

Ozga, S. Andrew. *Expectations in Economic Theory*, Chicago: Aldine Publishing Company, 1965.

Pouliquen, L. Y. *Risk Analysis in Project Appraisal*, World Bank Staff Occasional Paper No. 11.

Savage, L. J. *The Foundations of Statistics*. New York: John Wiley & Sons, 1954.

Swalm, Ralph O. "Utility Theory—Insights into Risk Taking," *Harvard Business Review*, November–December 1966.

von Neumann, J. and O. Morgenstern. *Theory of Games and Economic Behavior*. Princeton: Princeton University Press, 1947.

Wagle, A. "A Statistical Analysis of Risk in Capital Investment Projects," *Operational Research Quarterly*, Vol. 18, No. 1.

Zusman, P. and A. Amaid. "Farm Planning under Weather Uncertainty," *Journal of Farm Economics*, Vol. 14, August 1965.

7